DEDICATION

Since "JOY" is the theme of this study, its letters serve as a reminder of those to whom this work is dedicated —

"J" — to Jesus, the real JOY of my life!

"O" — to Others, who have so patiently and lovingly responded to this material when first presented, the body of believers at First Brethren Church of Long Beach, California.

"Y" — to You, my precious wife, Carole, for bringing me so much "joy" and for your constant example to me.

Table of Contents

1. A Church Is Born . . . Historical Background 9

PRINCIPLES OF JOY
No. 1 – The Philosophy of Your Life Must Be Centered in Jesus Christ

2. Your Attitudes Toward Other People 21
3. Your Acceptance of Difficult Places 33
4. Your Anticipation of Christ's Presence 43

PRINCIPLES OF JOY
No. 2 – The Pattern of Your Life Must be Conformed to Jesus Christ

5. Your Acknowledgment of Christ's Person 57
6. Your Application of God's Purposes 71
7. Your Appreciation of God's People 83

How To Be Happy
in Difficult Situations —

Studies

in

Philippians

How To Be Happy in Difficult Situations—

Studies in Philippians

David L. Hocking

BMH BOOKS
Winona Lake, Indiana

ISBN: 0-88469-027-X

COPYRIGHT 1975
BMH BOOKS
WINONA LAKE, INDIANA

Printed In U.S.A.

Unless otherwise designated, all Scripture passages and references are from the New American Standard Bible.

Words contained in parenthesis are from the Greek.

The ancient gateway on the cover is the entrance into the Roman city of Philippi. Photo by the author, David L. Hocking.

Cover design by Tim Kennedy.

PRINCIPLES OF JOY

No. 3 — The Purpose of Your Life Must Be
Controlled by Jesus Christ

✿✿✿✿✿

PRINCIPLES OF JOY

No. 4 — The Provision of Your Life Must Be
Complete in Christ

1

****

A Church Is Born—
Historical Background

****

THE CHAPTER OUTLINED:

I. The Call to Philippi

II. The First Converts in Europe

III. The Circumstances Leading to Imprisonment

IV. The Conversion of the Jailor

SUGGESTED BACKGROUND DEVOTIONAL READING

Monday—The Team of Paul and Silas (Acts 15:36-41)

Tuesday—The Selection of Timothy (Acts 16:1-5)

Wednesday—The Macedonian Call (Acts 16:6-10)

Thursday—First Converts in Europe (Acts 16:11-15)

Friday—Paul and Silas in Prison (Acts 16:16-24)

Saturday—A Jailor Is Saved (Acts 16:25-34)

Sunday—Leaving Town in Style (Acts 16:35-40)

The Apostle Paul was in the "church-planting" business from the time he left Antioch in Syria (Acts 13:1-4) until his death (II Tim. 4:6-8). Little groups of believers were developed in most of the major cities of the Roman world, and most of them were the result of this man's ministry. In terms of numbers, those churches would not seem great when compared with some of the "super-big" churches of our day (with the exception of the phenomenal growth and size of the church in Jerusalem), and yet, no matter the size, there is always something very exciting about the establishment of a new church! Philippi was no exception! Here was the first church established in mainland Europe!

It was my pleasure to visit the ruins of the ancient city of Philippi, and a little of that background is helpful when studying the 16th chapter of Acts which records Paul's first efforts in that city. At the northern end of the Aegean Sea (between Greece and Turkey) there is a beautiful little port city called Kavalla, which is the Neapolis of Bible times (Acts 16:11). Philippi is located inland from Neapolis about 10 miles. On the way to Philippi from Neapolis it is possible to see the remains of the ancient Roman roads; and to realize that long ago a man of God named Paul walked those same roads. Philippi was the "leading city of the district of Macedonia" according to Acts 16:12, and also a "Roman colony." Macedonia was divided into four districts in 168 B.C. when it fell into Roman hands. It could be that Philippi was the "chief (first) city" of one of those districts, for Thessalonica also seems to be some sort of a capital. The name of the city is attributed to Philip of Macedon, the father of Alexander the Great, who seized the city in 358 B.C., enlarged it, and made it a strong fortress. It was well situated in a very fertile plain surrounded by mountain ranges. It became a "Roman colony" shortly after 42 B.C. when Octavian (later became Emperor Augustus) and Antony were victorious over Brutus and Cassius on the plains outside the city. The city was granted immunity from taxation because of its significance and importance to the Roman armies.

There were no synagogues here, and the few Jewish residents would gather at the "river side" for prayer (Acts 16:13), of which most of the participants appear to be women. The present ruins of this ancient city date from the second century A.D. and as yet, the city of Paul's day has not been discovered.

THE CALL TO PHILIPPI — Acts 16:6-10

And they passed through the Phrygian and Galatian region, having been forbidden by the Holy Spirit to speak the word in Asia; and when they had come to Mysia, they were trying to go into Bithynia, and the Spirit of Jesus did not permit them; and passing by Mysia, they came down to Troas. And a vision appeared to Paul in the night: A certain man of Macedonia was standing and appealing to him, and saying, "Come over to Macedonia and help us." And when he had seen the vision, immediately we sought to go into Macedonia, concluding that God had called us to preach the gospel to them.

What a fascinating account of God's direction in a person's life! All of us need the kind of responsive heart that is revealed in these verses. Often, the Lord will simply close the door on our plans and the places we had decided to go. Too many times we become bitter, discouraged, and defeated over "closed doors" when it is simply the loving hand of a God who wants the very best for us and has a specific plan to work in our lives. It is difficult to say how the Spirit of God was impressing Paul's heart in these verses. Perhaps it was through circumstances. Maybe the roads into Bithynia were closed due to bad weather! Who knows? The obvious fact is that they were led by the Spirit of God.

We are told that "a vision appeared to Paul in the night." Was he awake or asleep? The words "in the night" seem to indicate that he was asleep and had a dream as we often do. However, before we start building a theological argument for "dreams and visions" as a chief way of God revealing His will today, remember that God did reveal things directly to the apostles, and that much of the New Testament revelation was not completed at this time. We now have the clear direction of God's Word, complete and final in its revelation, and adequate for all aspects of Christian life and practice.

The author William Ramsey (his book is entitled, *St. Paul the Traveller*) has an interesting view of this "man of Macedonia" who appeared to Paul in the vision. He argues that it is Luke, and that Philippi was his hometown. Before you cancel that thought out of your mind, it is interesting that a change in the use of pronouns occurs in Acts 16:10. Up to that verse, the text has been using the third person personal pronoun—"they," but in verse 10, there is a shift to the first person plural—"we." Since Luke is the writer of the Book of Acts, it appears that he joins the missionary team at this point and now writes about what he had actually experienced. Also, there is a question about how Paul would recognize this "man." Here is a reminder that God will often use other people to burden us with the need of going with the gospel message, regardless of who this "man" really is in Acts 16:9.

THE FIRST CONVERTS IN EUROPE — Acts 16:13-15

Can you remember the joy of sharing the Gospel for the first time as a new Christian? Have you ever had the joy of seeing the Lord work in a person's life to whom you have witnessed? What a thrill! No matter how long or how much you have shared the "good news" of Christ with others, it is always exciting to see someone give his heart to Christ! Paul had already enjoyed the fruit of his labors, but this was something special! It was the opening of the Gospel to Europe and the "heart" of the Roman Empire!

The amazing thing about this story is that Lydia was not a resident of Philippi, but of Thyatira which was located in Asia Minor (Turkey) across the Aegean Sea. Let's read the story of this conversion in Acts 16:13-15.

> And on the Sabbath day we went outside the gate to a river side, where we were supposing that there would be a place of prayer; and we sat down and began speaking to the women who had assembled. And a certain woman named Lydia, from the city of Thyatira, a seller of purple fabrics, a worshiper of God, was listening; and the Lord opened her heart to respond to the things spoken by Paul. And when she and her household had been baptized, she urged us, saying, "If you have judged me to be faithful to the Lord, come into my house and stay." And she prevailed upon us.

Thyatira was no doubt her original home, but perhaps for her business she had recently moved to Philippi where the Romans would be more responsive to the fine fabrics she was selling. At any rate, she had already established herself in Philippi with her family ("household" v. 15) and a place to live ("come into my house and stay" v. 15).

Two things of importance here in these verses: First, she appears to be a Jewish proselyte ("worshiper of God"), who along with some other women were being faithful to God on the Sabbath Day even though there was no synagogue in that city. Second, it is marvelous to read the words, "and the Lord opened her heart to respond to the things spoken by Paul." It is God who opens hearts! When people respond to our message and witness, do not forget that it is because God is working in them and causing this response.

THE CIRCUMSTANCES LEADING TO IMPRISONMENT —
Acts 16:16-24

When Paul wrote Philippians he was in jail; when Paul was in Philippi he was in jail! Someone has said that when Paul went to a new city he did not ask what the hotels were like, but rather what the jails were like since he usually wound up there anyway! We will understand the message of Philippians much better when we realize the circumstances under which Paul wrote and under which he labored when he was in Philippi.

The problem arose regarding this demon-possessed slave girl who was bringing her owners "much profit by fortune-telling" (v. 16). Times haven't changed much, because it is still a profit-making business! Now, what she said was not all that bad. In verse 17 we read, "These men are bond-servants of the Most High God, who are proclaiming to you the way of salvation." But Paul wasn't too thrilled with the sponsorship and advertisement of this girl! Verse 18 states that after "many days," Paul finally turned to the girl ("greatly annoyed") and said to the spirit, "I command you in the name of Jesus Christ to come out of her!" And, of course, the evil spirit came out immediately. "Casting out demons" is one of the miraculous "signs" that Jesus predicted would be used by the apostles to "confirm" the spoken Word (cf. Mark 16:17-20; Heb. 2:3-4). Well, the owners, being motivated by the profit/loss game, were not too happy about this turn of affairs, and as a result, Paul and Silas were dragged into the marketplace before the "chief magistrates" of that city. The charge against them was not casting out a demon, but teaching customs which Romans could not accept or observe. It was purely a mob in action, with no real trial. They ripped off their robes, beat them with rods, and threw them into prison with their feet in the "stocks." When I visited ancient Philippi, the remains are there of what appears to be an ancient prison. There is some question as to whether it is the one Paul and Silas were in, but, nevertheless, it was a moving experience to stand in that little prison and remember the occasion of Acts 16. On the wall of that prison, a beautiful little plaque has been placed with the words of Philippians 1:21 on it: "For to me to live is Christ; and to die is gain."

THE CONVERSION OF THE JAILOR – Acts 16:25-34

No believer can read this story without getting excited about God's power and His marvelous ways in the lives of people! Who would have thought that a Roman jailor, rough and mean in temperament, language, dress, culture, and actions, would have been gloriously saved! God can save anyone, no matter how severe their background or great their sin! Praise God for His wonderful love to all men and His gracious forgiveness! First a gracious, refined, businesslike woman becomes a believer, and then—a

Roman jailor! Now there's a church for you!

When you read this story, the first thing that hits you with great impact is the *attitude* of Paul and Silas in the midst of very difficult circumstances. Verse 25 states, "But about midnight Paul and Silas were praying and singing hymns of praise to God, and the prisoners were listening to them." That's the result of being filled with the Spirit (cf. Eph. 5:18-21). Most of us, our backs bruised and bleeding, our bodies cramped by the awkward position of the stocks, our future at the best uncertain, would begin to complain, cry, and ask—"Why me? Lord." Knowing what the Bible says about testings, the Lord would have every right to answer, "Why not you?" But, we read of no such complaining in the lives of these two servants of God. What a tremendous example for all of us to follow! Philippians is about JOY! No wonder after this experience in the jail of Philippi that Paul could write what he did in the Book of Philippians! Here's a man who practiced what he preached! He knew what it was to experience suffering for the cause of Christ, and to have the joy of the Lord in the midst of it all!

In addition to the marvelous *attitude* which Paul and Silas displayed, there is immediate *acceptance* on the part of the prisoners. Verse 25 reads, "and the prisoners were listening." The word used for "listening" in the original language carries the idea of hearing with favor. You don't normally hear such things in a prison! The verb suggests the idea of continuity—"they were continuing to listen."

> And suddenly there came a great earthquake, so that the foundations of the prison-house were shaken; and immediately all the doors were opened, and everyone's chains were unfastened. And when the jailer had been roused out of sleep and had seen the prison doors opened, he drew his sword and was about to kill himself, supposing that the prisoners had escaped (Acts 16:26-27).

Circumstances can seem pretty difficult at times and awfully discouraging, and then a simple *act* of God changes everything! It is nothing to God to cause an earthquake. Psalm 148:8 states that He is in control of the forces of nature and they are fulfilling His Word! Praise the Lord!

At the point when the jailer was ready to "end it all," Paul brought the amazing news that none of the prisoners had escaped. One of the most touching scenes in the Bible and most reflective of the grace of God is recorded in verses 29 and 30 as this rough, old jailer is humbled by the power of God.

> And he called for lights and rushed in and trembling with fear, he fell

down before Paul and Silas, and after he brought them out, he said,
"Sirs, what must I do to be saved?"

That's what I would call *asking* the right question! This was no time for a
lengthy discourse; it was time for the simple Gospel. We need to learn
when unbelievers are prepared by God's Holy Spirit and need only the
simple message as to how they can be saved. And what an *answer*! Verse
31 says, "Believe in the Lord Jesus, and you shall be saved, you and your
household." The "household" would not be saved just because the jailer
was saved, but they could be saved in the same way—by believing in the
Lord Jesus. Paul opened the door to reaching the man's entire family. As
verse 32 states, Paul did go to his house and speak the word of the Lord to
all of them. At the jailer's home we already see a display of conversion as
the jailer washes their wounds, and he and his household are baptized.
They didn't waste any time in following through with their commitment
to Christ by being baptized. It reminds us of the situation in Acts 2:41
where 3,000 people were baptized "in that day."

> And he brought them into his house and set food before them, and
> rejoiced greatly, having believed in God with his whole household"
> (Acts 16:34).

Again, we are reminded of the theme of Philippians—"Joy" or "rejoicing." The jailer and his whole family are now believers and they are happy
in the Lord. The suffering was worth it all as Paul and Silas sat down to eat
with these new babes in Christ. A church was being built! What wonderful
confirmation of that vision they had back at Troas! God was giving them
assurance and confidence of His leading in their lives.

> Now when day came, the chief magistrates sent their policemen, saying,
> "Release those men." And the jailer reported these words to Paul,
> saying, "The chief magistrates have sent to release you. Now therefore
> come out and go in peace." But Paul said to them, "They have beaten
> us in public without trial, men who are Romans, and have thrown us
> into prison; and now are they sending us away secretly? No indeed! But
> let them come themselves and bring us out." And the policemen re-
> ported these words to the chief magistrates. And they were afraid when
> they heard that they were Romans, and they came and appealed to
> them, and when they had brought them out, they kept begging them to
> leave the city. And they went out of the prison and entered the house
> of Lydia, and when they saw the brethren, they encouraged them and
> departed (Acts 16:35-40).

The word for "chief magistrates" in the original language was used of
those who were in charge of towns which were Roman colonies. Under-

neath them were "serjeants" or "lictors" who would execute their orders. These men had obviously violated Roman law in punishing Paul and Silas without trial, due to the fact that they were Roman citizens, entitled to the protection of the law. Their job was now threatened, and they tried to get Paul and Silas to leave quietly, hoping that the word would not get back to Rome.

It's in this situation that we see an interesting side of the life and character of Paul. Most of us would have been glad for the opportunity to get out of town as fast as we could! But not Paul! He had been through enough already and was not afraid to suffer for his Lord. He took advantage of the situation and used the opportunity to leave the city in style, and only after he had spent time with this new little group of believers.

The two problems that Paul presented to the policemen who were sent by the chief magistrates were serious matters. One dealt with the issue of being beaten "in public." The word in Greek is the root behind our word "democracy," meaning the "people." It was never right to take a Roman citizen and punish him in front of the people without a trial. It was considered to be a disgrace and shame. The second issue was concerned with being beaten "without trial." This whole affair was "not according to judgment." The "judgment" would deal with the grounds upon which the beating could have taken place. There was no official trial, charge, or judgment given. This also was a serious violation of Roman law. From verse 39, we can see the seriousness of this action on the part of the chief magistrates. They came personally this time to Paul and Silas, and the text says "they kept begging them to leave the city." No longer is it an order from them, but a continual pleading and begging. Paul could have been very vindictive here and have reported them to Rome, but we do not read of such an attitude.

What a joy to read verse 40 when it says, "they saw the brethren." The word "brethren" is the affectionate word used of believers in the New Testament. Here was the nucleus of a new church. Its first meeting place was the home of Lydia, and no doubt the jailer and his family were there also. It was my privilege to experience the same thing in seeing a church born and meet in a house. It was exciting to gather with a few believers in a home and experience the closeness and warmth of fellowship in Christ! One always hated to leave those wonderful occasions of fellowship, especially when the room was filled with new babes in Christ, hungry for the Word of God! The text says, "they encouraged them." The word is the same as the word "comforter." It means "one called alongside of." It is translated "encouragement," "consolation," and "comfort." Sometimes it takes a stronger meaning, like "exhortation" or "counsel." It is listed as one of the spiritual gifts in Romans 12:8. Paul and Silas did their best to encourage these new believers before departing from them. They knew that these new babes in Christ would soon be facing many trials and difficulties, and without leadership, it would be very difficult. But, they also knew that God would raise up the leadership necessary for this new church. Evidently, that had already occurred by the time of his writing the Book of Philippians because chapter 1, verse 1, of that book records that there were "bishops and deacons" in the church.

The tendency of the new convert is to become discouraged and not to continue in the faith. He gets away from the Word (which contains "the faith once and for all delivered unto the saints"—Jude 3), and his trials become sources of irritation and defeat rather than keys to maturity and spiritual development. Much of the Book of Philippians seems to underscore this need in the lives of believers. We need to realize that our suffering and trials are building us to maturity, and for this, we can say with James 1:2-4:

> Consider it all joy, my brethren, when you encounter various trials; knowing that the testing of your faith produces endurance. And let endurance have its perfect result, that you may be perfect and complete, lacking in nothing.

There is "joy" in the midst of trial when we understand God's purposes and realize what He is accomplishing in our lives.

Philippians is a book of joy, but also of suffering. The two are beautifully woven together, and best seen in the life of the writer, Paul, who through much tribulation, demonstrated the qualities of one who truly had joy and was always rejoicing. Acts 16 tells us of that example and the background of the Book of Philippians. But, in addition to that story, Paul's life continued to demonstrate the truths he taught in Philippians. And even while writing the book, he again was in the midst of great trial but could say as he did in chapter 4, "Rejoice in the Lord always; again I will say, rejoice!"

STUDY QUESTIONS:

1. What persuaded Paul and Silas that God wanted them to go to Philippi?

2. What factors were involved in preparing the heart of Lydia for the message of the Gospel?

3. What was the immediate situation that resulted in the imprisonment of Paul and Silas?

4. What did you learn from the attitude of Paul and Silas while they were in prison?

Principles of Joy

+++

PRINCIPLE NO. 1

THE PHILOSOPHY OF YOUR LIFE
MUST BE CENTERED IN JESUS CHRIST

Philippians 1:1-30

KEY VERSE: Philippians 1:21—"For to me, to live is Christ, and to die is gain."

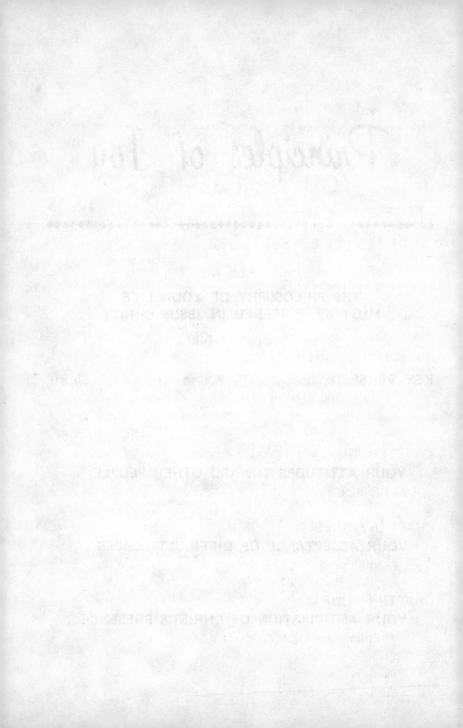

✝✝✝

Your Attitudes Toward Other People

✝✝✝

THE CHAPTER OUTLINED:

    I. **Giving Praise to God for Others**
       A. His continual acknowledgment of them in prayer to God
       B. His close association with them in the work of the Gospel
       C. His constant affection for them

    II. **Offering Prayer to God for Others**
       A. Prayer for an abundance of love
       B. Prayer for and approval of excellent things
       C. Prayer for an affluence of righteousness

SUGGESTED BACKGROUND DEVOTIONAL READING

Monday—Thanking God for Others (Col. 1:1-8)

Tuesday—What to Pray (Col. 1:9-14)

Wednesday—The Joy of Being in Jail (Philemon 1:8-20)

Thursday—Learning to Praise God (Ps. 100)

Friday—Abundant Love (I John 4:7-21)

Saturday—Producing Fruit (John 15:1-8)

Sunday—Joy in Loving (John 15:9-16)

PRINCIPLES OF JOY

The first of the four principles of joy that we will study in this wonderful Book of Philippians is found in chapter 1, with the key verse being verse 21: *The philosophy of your life must be centered in Jesus Christ!* Key verse: "For to me, to live is Christ, and to die is gain."

To have joy, one must realize that his philosophy—how he thinks, believes, and understands, is affecting him. The Apostle Paul shares this principle with us in three primary ways in this chapter. Our philosophy will involve these three things if we are to experience joy in our Christian life.

1. It involves *your attitudes toward other people* (Phil. 1:1-11)

2. It involves *your acceptance of difficult places* (Phil. 1:12-21).

3. It involves *your anticipation of Christ's presence* (Phil. 1:22-30).

Our present discussion will center around verses 1-11 dealing with our attitudes toward other people. There are two basic thoughts in these verses as to our attitudes toward others:

1. In giving *praise* to God for others—1:3-8

2. In offering *prayer* to God for others—1:9-11

These two things could revolutionize your life in terms of your relationships with other people, and thus bring real joy to you. Much of the unhappiness we experience as believers is related to how we get along with other people!

OPENING REMARKS AND GREETINGS — 1:1-2

> Paul and Timothy, bond-servants of Christ Jesus, to all the saints in Christ Jesus who are in Philippi, including the overseers and deacons: Grace to you and peace from God our Father and the Lord Jesus Christ.

The first thing that is drawn to our attention as we begin to read this little letter of joy is the fact that Paul and Timothy refer to themselves as "bond-servants of Christ Jesus." The word in Greek (*douloi*) was characteristic of Paul—like a favorite term. The basic fact behind it was that of total submission of the individual to his owner or master. It was the direct opposite of the great desire of the Greeks—freedom. Christ even referred to Himself as a "bond-servant" in Philippians 2:7. A "bond-servant [or slave]" had no rights of his own. His will was the will of his master. What impact this ought to have upon all of us who claim to be "servants of Jesus

Christ"! No wonder that many of us have no joy in our experience when we do not submit to the authority and control of Jesus Christ! The one great passion of Paul's life was to do God's will—no matter what it cost him! On the Damascus road (Acts 9:5-6) when Paul cried out "Who art Thou, Lord?" he received the answer, "it shall be told you what you must do."

The second thing that strikes us with importance in the greeting to the church is that the recipients of the letter are called "saints in Christ Jesus" (v. 1). An additional note is given when it says, "including the overseers and deacons." The letter was not written to the overseers and deacons, but to the saints *with* the overseers and deacons. We can learn much from the way this phrase is constructed. The "saints" include the "overseers" and "deacons." All believers are called "saints." The word translated "including" (*sun*) indicates there was a close companionship and fellowship between the leaders and the church body as a whole.

The basic structure of a local church is being revealed here in this verse. It is composed of believers or "saints" of which some are chosen to be bishops or "overseers" and some to be "deacons." The plural form of "bishops" and "deacons" would seem to argue for at least two or more in the basic structure of the church. This verse would also seem to indicate that "bishops" or "overseers" were confined to the ministry of the local church rather than superintending a larger area, district, or province with many churches involved. The term "overseer" means "to look over or upon." The term seems to be synonymous with the term "elder" and "pastor" (shepherd) as seen in passages like Acts 20:17, 28 and I Peter 5:1-4. In addition to the "overseers" we have the mention of "deacons." The word means "one who serves." Most commentators believe that the origin of this office is found in Acts 6 where seven men are chosen by the congregation at Jerusalem to assist the apostles and to relieve them of various support tasks so that they could give themselves to the Word of God and prayer. The true function of a deacon is service. Leadership and direction in the affairs of the local church were centered in the "bishop" or "elder."

The basic desire of Paul and Timothy toward the church at Philippi was that they might be recipients of "grace" and "peace" from the Father and from Jesus Christ. This, of course, was the common greeting of Paul in his letters. The exact word order of Philippians 1:2 is found in Romans, I and II Corinthians, Galatians, Ephesians, II Thessalonians, and Philemon. Very similar words are found in Colossians, I Thessalonians, I and II Timothy, and Titus. Some believe that these words are nothing more than ancient greetings. "Grace" would refer to the Greek way of greeting, and "peace" to the Jewish way. But the emphasis upon the joint source of these two words—"from God our Father and Lord Jesus Christ"—would seem to indicate more of spiritual blessing than of mere social greeting. The teaching of Paul regarding the doctrine of "grace" and of "peace" is so frequent in his writings that we cannot help but believe that he is referring to the spiritual qualities primarily. "Grace" must always precede "peace." And, there is no "grace" apart from our Lord Jesus Christ. I have in my library a set of notes by the late Dr. Alva J. McClain of a series he preached in 1920 on the Book of Philippians. He wrote concerning this greeting:

> You may search the Word of God but you will never find peace first—it is always "*grace* and peace"—never "peace and grace." They are the Siamese twins of the Bible. You cannot have peace until you first have had grace. A man may search and seek until the end of his life, but until he receives grace through Christ, he can never have peace. I was wondering if we could find grace extended to the Christian without the name of Christ, but—never, from greeting to benediction, in all the Word of God have I found grace apart from Jesus Christ. His name is always there.

I. GIVING PRAISE TO GOD FOR OTHERS — 1:3-8

The first way in which we can experience joy in our attitudes toward others is by learning to praise God for other people. That's the secret of Paul's joy as discovered in verses 3 to 8:

> I thank my God in all my remembrance of you, always offering prayer with joy in my every prayer for you all, in view of your participation in the gospel from the first day until now. For I am confident of this very thing, that He who began a good work in you will perfect it until the day of Christ Jesus. For it is only right for me to feel this way about you all, because I have you in my heart, since both in my imprisonment and in the defense and confirmation of the gospel, you all are partakers of grace with me. For God is my witness, how I long for you all with the affection of Christ Jesus."

There were three things affecting this continual attitude of praise in his heart to God:

A. His continual acknowledgment of them in prayer to God — 1:3-4

B. His close association with them in the work of the Gospel — 1:5-6

C. His constant affection for them — 1:7-8

These things could change many of our lives in terms of our attitudes toward other people. Let's examine them in some detail.

A. His continual acknowledgment of them in prayer to God — 1:3-4

If you are praying for people by name, it is definitely going to make a difference in how you relate to them and to their needs. In examining the manner in which Paul prayed, three statements stand out: The first is the expression of thanks—"I thank my God." The Greek word (*eucharisto*) comes from the word for "grace" and the word "well" or "good." The communion elements of the bread and wine were taken after Jesus had "given thanks," and they have often been called the Eucharist, which means "giving thanks." It is very difficult to have much joy in our relationships with others if we do not learn to give thanks to God for them. A continual habit of giving thanks to God is suggested here.

The second word dealing with the manner in which Paul prayed is the word translated "prayer" in verse 4. The Greek word (*deesei*) is often translated "supplication," and refers to the existence or expression of a particular need. Paul was praying for God to meet their needs. Praying for the needs of others also makes us more sensitive to people and more concerned for them.

The third word or statement that emphasizes the manner in which Paul prayed are the words "with joy." Literally, the text reads, "with joy making the prayer." The question might be, which came first, the joy or the prayer? Did Paul's possession of joy affect his prayer, or did his prayer life affect his joy? Both would certainly be true, but the context seems to indicate that Paul was motivated toward prayer in their behalf because his remembrance of them brought joy to his heart due to their participation with him in the work of the Gospel. We should certainly pray for all believers regardless of their response, but it sure helps when they are serving the Lord!

The method by which he was motivated to pray for them is stated in the phrase of verse 3, "in all my remembrance of you." Whenever the Lord brought them to his attention, he prayed for them. We all ought to learn to do this—when the Lord brings someone to your attention, pray for them!

B. His close association with them in the work of the Gospel — 1:5-6

The second fact that affected his attitude of praise for these believers was his close association with them in the work of the Gospel. In examining *the participation they had with him,* there are two possible viewpoints of what Paul was referring to in the phrase "in view of your participation in the gospel" (v. 5). Some would say that it is referring to their salvation. Thus, he would be praying with joy knowing that they were his converts and had truly been saved. Others would refer this to their fellowship with Paul in sharing the Gospel with others. In the light of what he goes on to say in verse 12, and following, about his work in spreading the Gospel in Rome, it would seem that this latter view is the better one. Thus, the thing that brought joy to Paul's heart was the knowledge that these believers in Philippi had been active in sharing the "good news" of Christ, and thus were "fellowshipping" (the word means "that which we share in common") with Paul.

In verse 5, we notice also that they had displayed *a pattern of faithfulness* in sharing the Gospel with others. The text says, "from the first day until now." This would remind us of the historical background of Acts 16. What a wonderful thing to say about a group of believers! They had been faithful in witnessing since the day they received Christ!

In verse 6, we see the basic reason why Paul had so much joy and praise in his heart toward them. His confidence was in God! *The persuasion in his heart* was based on what God will do. His confidence was not in their ability to stay with it, or continue to perform; it was in the Lord's ability and performance of His will in them. The word "confident" in verse 6 could be translated, "having been persuaded." It began when they became believers; Paul saw that it was real and was so persuaded; it had continued through the years, and by the time he wrote this epistle, his confidence had remained. This persuasion was based upon two things: First, it was based upon God's *activity* at and in their salvation. The words "He who began a good work in you" express Paul's confidence in the Lord at the moment of their conversion. The word "to begin" combines with the preposition "in" and emphasizes that God worked their salvation within them. "He who began" means that God did it in and of Himself! Salvation is truly of God, not man! As John 1:13 puts it: "Who were born not of blood, nor of the will of the flesh, nor of the will of man, but of God." It is not by physical descent, nor the desire of our own hearts, nor by the deeds of others that we are saved—it is solely of God!

Paul's persuasion was also based upon God's *ability* to complete what He started. Verse 6 says, "will perfect it until the day of Christ Jesus." The word "perfect" combines a common word meaning "to fulfill, complete, finish, end," plus the preposition "upon" which would emphasize the completeness of the process. The meaning then is that God will accomplish *completely* what He started! The words "until the day of Christ Jesus" would seem to refer to the second coming of Christ. I John 3:2 emphasizes that when we see Him we shall be "like Him." The process which began in us at our conversion will then be completed. Paul spoke of this in Romans 8:23 as "the redemption of our body" which the whole creation is awaiting.

The third fact that affected his attitude of praise for these believers was rooted deep within his heart.

C. His constant affection for them – 1:7-8

A key phrase of this section and a basic principle of having the joy of the Lord in our attitudes toward other people is "I have you in my heart." Paul's constant affection for them was based on three things. First, it was based upon the *regard* he had for them in his heart. If you think right toward people, you will act right! The words "to feel this way" are from the word "to think." He was always responding with joy. It was only "right" or "proper" for him to be thinking this about these believers because they were in his heart. He had a deep affection for them that would not pass away. It was not an affection for a limited few either. He said it was "about you all" or "in the behalf of all of you." He was not excluding anyone. He loved them all! What an example to all of us! Here was a man filled with the love of Christ! He who hated and persecuted the Christians early in his life is now deeply in love with them! When someone is really in your heart (or, under your skin!), this condition will produce the response that Paul was experiencing.

His affection was also based upon certain specific *reasons* which he gave. One dealt with his "bonds." He was referring to his imprisonment. He was in jail in Rome at this time, and he was also in jail when he was at Philippi. The fellow believers were partakers with Paul at this time. They shared with him in his needs, and it brought much joy to his heart. Second, he spoke of "the defense and confirmation of the gospel." His "defense" (*apologia* from which we get our word "apology") and "confirmation" are legal terms dealing with his trial and his answer to those who had brought charges against him which caused him to be in prison at this time. Paul spoke in II Timothy 4:16: "At my first defense no one supported me, but all deserted me; may it not be counted against them." This dealt with his final imprisonment from which he did not escape. No one stood by him then. However, it was not so in this case in Philippians 1:7. These Philippian believers stood by him and shared with him in his time of need. No wonder he loved them! He says that "you all are partakers of grace with me." He calls both of these things ("bonds" and "defense and confirmation") the result of God's grace. He saw these things not as hindrances or trials, but as blessings and exciting opportunities for the advancement of the Gospel of Christ!

His affection was also based upon his *relationship* to Jesus Christ. The real reason behind all that he says in these opening verses is not that he was such an outstanding person or knew how to love people himself, but that he had encountered the marvelous love and compassion of Christ. In verse 8 he emphasizes his sincerity in this by stating: "For God is my witness." The point being that if he was lying about these deep feelings that he was expressing, then he was accountable to God. He wanted them to know how deeply he felt toward them.

The words "I long for you all" stress two important things: One, the intensity of his feelings. The word "long for" is another word that combines with a preposition giving it intensity. The meaning is a "great longing." Second, the verb is in the present tense indicating a continual habit of life. He was constantly feeling this for them. It wasn't just a momentary thought that crossed his mind. He had deep feelings for them. The sphere in which he felt all of this longing he calls "bowels [KJV—the NASV has "affection"] of Jesus Christ." The word translated "affection" or "bowels" is a word referring to the physical organs of intestines. The Greeks used the word as the seat of violent passion. The Jews used it as the seat of tender affections. It is used of Christ frequently in the Gospels (Matt. 9:36; 14:14; 15:32; 18:27; 20:34; Mark 1:41; 6:34; 8:2; 9:22) and stresses the deep compassion He felt for both the multitudes as well as the individual. He felt this way in seeing the multitudes like sheep without a shepherd, when He saw the sick needing to be healed, when He saw them hungry and in need of food, and when He saw one person, like a leper, who needed help. The word emphasizes the deep feeling inside a person that aches because you care so much for the other person. Oh, how we need the touch of this compassion upon our lives! No wonder Paul loved these people so much! He had experienced the love and compassion of Christ.

II. OFFERING PRAYER TO GOD FOR OTHERS — 1:9-11

And this I pray, that your love may abound still more and more in real

knowledge and all discernment, so that you may approve the things
that are excellent, in order to be sincere and blameless until the day of
Christ; having been filled with the fruit of righteousness which comes
through Jesus Christ, to the glory and praise of God.

The first way in which our attitudes toward other people is affected in
having joy is in giving praise to God for others (vv. 3-8). Now we come to
the second way which is in offering prayer to God for others. If we expect
our attitudes toward others to be proper and joyful, we must examine the
nature of what we pray for in their behalf. It is always a little embarrassing
to study the prayers of Paul in the Bible when you realize how little we
pray in that way. It is important to bring our specific needs to God in
prayer like sickness, job, food, money, activities, and so forth. However,
Paul seems to emphasize the spiritual qualities which are needed in a
person's life.

Notice that verse 9 begins with the words: "And *this* I [Paul] pray."
The word "pray" indicates a continual pattern of life. He was constantly
in prayer for them. Jesus said "Men ought always to pray and not to faint"
(Luke 18:1). Paul wrote in I Thessalonians 5:17, "Pray without ceasing."
He practiced what he preached! The word "this" seems to indicate there is
one main request in verses 9-11 that is being emphasized, rather than four
requests as is often brought out. The one request would be for their love
to abound more and more in knowledge and in all discernment. The rest of
the phrases or clauses seem to develop that point, each flowing out of the
one that preceded it. Also, the words "in order that" do not appear before
each of what seems to be four phrases, but is listed only twice. For the
benefit of study, we will consider each of the four lines of thought sepa-
rately as parts of his prayer although as we have said, it appears to be a
prayer for love.

A. Prayer for an abundance of love – v. 9

. . . that your love may abound still more and more in real knowledge
and all discernment.

The *development* of this love in their lives is described in two basic
ways: First, there is an emphasis upon the *extent* of this love. That is
found in the words "may abound." This might refer to our love reaching
many people, abounding to many. Paul prayed that their love might extend out to all kinds of people. Second, there is an emphasis upon the
effectiveness of that love when it touches other peoples' lives. The words
"still more and more" emphasize this thought.

As we all know, there are many different interpretations of love and expressions of love. Are there any guidelines for us in the exercise of Christian love? Absolutely! The *definition* of how this abundant love should be expressed is found in the qualifying words "in real knowledge and all discernment." The word for "knowledge" indicates full, mature knowledge. The emphasis is upon a complete understanding of how love operates, and what it is like when you experience it. That understanding comes through the knowledge of God's Word. We don't have that mature knowledge apart from God's revelation.

The second word "discernment" is very important in the exercise of love. While the next phrase will qualify it more, the meaning is moral perception. In the Septuagint (Greek Old Testament) this word appears in Proverbs 1:22 and 2:10 where we observe that fools hate it. One of the prime examples of the fool in the early chapters of Proverbs was his lack of moral discernment. Sometimes we may feel a deep affection for someone, but it doesn't make it right to express it in any way we like. There are moral and ethical considerations that govern the exercise of an abundant love. Obviously, that moral discernment is also based on the knowledge of God's Word, the only true standard of morality in the world today.

B. Prayer for and approval of excellent things – v. 10

So that you may approve the things that are excellent.

The explanation of moral discernment in love is now given when he uses the term "excellent things." First, let's notice the *responsibility* we have. The verse reads, "so that you may approve." What does it mean to "approve"? The word was used with reference to the testing of metals. The emphasis would be the testing of what is right in this matter of love. That testing would precede the approval. The "testing" process would be the careful examination of the Word of God as to what principles would guide us in the expression of our love. What does the Bible permit or prohibit? That is the real question. It is not simply what we feel, but what is right according to the Word of God.

The second important thing about this approval deals with the *recognition* of what is "excellent." This word comes from a word meaning "to bear or carry" and the preposition "through." The point would be that the things that bear through the testing (what the Word says about them) we would approve. It would be the things that meet the conditions of having full, mature knowledge and moral discernment. The word often means "to differ" or "carry different ways." The Bible is the only sure guide in determining the difference in various actions and expressions of love as to what is right.

C. Prayer for an absence of hypocrisy — v. 10

> . . . in order to be sincere and blameless until the day of Christ.

This possible hypocrisy happens when we express our love in the wrong way, not following the principles of God's Word. It will bring all sorts of problems to us in terms of our effectiveness and testimony before others. The word "sincere" (*eilikrineis*) is translated in I Corinthians 5:8 as "un-leavened" in referring to bread. It was used of unmixed substances. The emphasis is upon moral and ethical purity. Some refer this word to a process of examining the quality of a piece of pottery by exposing it to the sunlight. If the substance of the piece of pottery was pure and un-mixed, it would be described as "sincere." We should make sure that in the expression of our love there is no mixture of sinful desires and wrong motives.

The word "blameless" (*aproskopoi*) is not referring to the words "without spot or blemish," but it rather refers to not causing anyone to stumble. However, the word here in Philippians 1:10 which is translated "blameless" is pointing to the ever-present danger of expressing love in the wrong way, and thus causing another brother or sister to stumble. If we cause one to stumble, how can we say that it was the love of Christ controlling us (cf. I Cor. 8:9-13)? The text emphasizes that we should maintain this absence of hypocrisy "until the day of Christ." Again, it is referring to the second coming of Jesus Christ. John wrote in I John 3:3, "And every one who has this hope fixed on Him purifies himself, just as He is pure."

D. Prayer for an affluence of righteousness — v. 11

> . . . having been filled with the fruit of righteousness which comes through Jesus Christ, to the glory and praise of God.

This would describe the *manner* in which we can be sincere and blame-less in our love. If we are filled with the fruit of Christ's righteousness, then we will be "sincere" and "blameless" in the expression of our love. The "fruit of righteousness" is not referring to our own righteousness, but that of Christ. Christ always expresses an abundance of love toward people and always in the right way. The *motivation* behind all of this is expressed in the last phrase of verse 11—"to the glory and praise of God." Whatever we do or say should all be to the glory of God. The word "praise" is only used of God. We were designed to give glory and praise to Him (Rev. 4:11). May it be so in every expression of our love to others. It will be if it is the love of Christ we are expressing.

The philosophy of our lives must be centered in Jesus Christ if we are to experience joy. This involves our attitudes toward other people. Those attitudes will be affected by two things: One, in giving praise to God for others; and, two, in offering prayer to God for others. Paul's example is outstanding and quite a challenge to all of us. Remember his words, "I have you in my heart." Is that how we feel about others?

STUDY QUESTIONS:

1. What is the meaning of the word "bond-servant [slave]"?

2. What things about Paul's prayer life were important to you in this passage?

3. Upon what was Paul's confidence (persuasion) based according to verse 6?

4. What was the main reason why Paul had such deep feelings and longing in his heart for these people?

5. What is the main thing for which Paul prayed for them?

6. What qualifications should we place upon the expression of love in our lives?

3 PHILIPPIANS 1:12-21

++

Your Acceptance
of Difficult Places

++

THE CHAPTER OUTLINED:

   I. **Accepting Your Circumstances**
      A. The reason
      B. The results

   II. **Accepting Your Conflicts**

   III. **Accepting Your Chance to Exalt Jesus Christ**
      A. This chance to exalt Jesus was based upon Paul's expectation
      B. The extent of this commitment

SUGGESTED BACKGROUND DEVOTIONAL READING

Monday—Learning to Suffer (I Peter 4:12-19)

Tuesday—God Uses Suffering (I Peter 3:8-15)

Wednesday—Why We Suffer (II Cor. 1:3-7)

Thursday—Difficult Circumstances in Asia (II Cor. 1:8-11)

Friday—Looking at Eternal Values (II Cor. 4:7-18)

Saturday—The Blessing of Others (II Tim. 1:8-18)

Sunday—No Reason To Be Afraid (II Tim. 4:1-8)

YOUR ACCEPTANCE OF DIFFICULT PLACES — 1:12-21

Chapter 1 of Philippians is emphasizing the first principle of joy—"The philosophy of your life must be centered in Jesus Christ." This involves your attitudes toward other people, which we examined in our last chapter from verses 1 to 11. We now come to the second thing that is involved in a philosophy that brings joy to your life.

> Now I want you to know, brethren, that my circumstances have turned out for the greater progress of the gospel, so that my imprisonment in the cause of Christ has become well-known throughout the whole praetorian guard and to everyone else, and that most of the brethren, trusting in the Lord because of my imprisonment, have far more courage to speak the word of God without fear. Some, to be sure, are preaching Christ even from envy and strife, but some also from good will; the latter do it out of love, knowing that I am appointed for the defense of the gospel; the former proclaim Christ out of selfish ambition, rather than from pure motives, thinking to cause me distress in my imprisonment. What then? Only that in every way, whether in pretense or in truth, Christ is proclaimed; and in this I rejoice, yes, and I will rejoice. For I know that this shall turn out for my deliverance through your prayers and the provision of the Spirit of Jesus Christ, according to my earnest expectation and hope, that I shall not be put to shame in anything, but that with all boldness, Christ shall even now, as always, be exalted in my body, whether by life or by death. For to me, to live is Christ, and to die is gain.

The circumstances of life are not always to our choosing, nor do we understand at times why we are experiencing them. Often we complain instead of rejoice. We view things as hindrances to our plans, unnecessary burdens or trials to face, upsetting situations, and events that we certainly do not deserve! Frequently we ask, "Why did this happen to me?" Sometimes those circumstances become just too much to bear, and we fall into deep depression and discouragement. Often we give up, believing that it is just not worth it all. Some people become bitter when the circumstances of life go the opposite way from that which they planned. Rebellion toward authority (especially God's!), bitterness toward others, hostility toward various responsibilities and people, and all kinds of hatred and anger begin to pour out of their lives. The simplest and most frequent response to changing circumstances is discouragement. We are disappointed that plans did not turn out like we thought.

But where are the people who are praising the Lord in all this? Where are those who are excited with what God is doing? Here's one—Paul! He accepted his circumstances as being from the hand of God. He knew by experience the words he wrote in Romans 8:28, "And we know that God causes all things to work together for good to those who love God, to those who are called according to His purpose." That's right—*"all things"!* There are three basic principles to guide us in this section of Scripture as to living above your circumstances:

I.   Accepting your circumstances as being used of God to further His plan in your life—1:12-14.

II. Accepting your conflicts with others as being from the Lord for your good — 1:15-19.

III. Accepting your chance to exalt Jesus Christ no matter what happens to you — 1:20-21.

These principles could radically change our attitudes and our abilities in living above our circumstances and in learning to interpret them in the light of God's will and plan.

I. ACCEPTING YOUR CIRCUMSTANCES AS BEING USED OF GOD TO FURTHER HIS PLAN IN YOUR LIFE — 1:12-14

Remind yourself again of Paul's situation. He is in Rome facing trial. He's in jail again! He is not facing this trial for the first time—he's been there before! He knows what ancient jails are like—from the inside! It's not very pleasant, even though his circumstances in Rome on this occasion were quite a bit different from the cold dungeon-like atmosphere of the Mamertine Prison where he found himself when writing the book of II Timothy (his last).

A. The reason God brought these circumstances into his life.

> Now I want you to know, brethren, that my circumstances have turned out for the greater progress of the gospel (1:12).

The first reason he gave is found in the beginning phrase, "Now I want you to know, brethren." It was to *encourage* the believers. The word "want" refers to "desire" or "counsel." It indicates a definite plan. He knew that these believers needed to understand why God had allowed these circumstances to occur. The second reason was to *extend* the Gospel in other places—"my circumstances have turned out for the greater progress of the gospel." The words "turned out" literally mean "have come" or "arrived." It is in the perfect tense meaning that they not only began at a certain point in the past, but they continue at the present time.

It seems like Paul's life was one constant example of how circumstances that appear to be trials and difficulties are turned into blessings and especially into further expansion of the Gospel of Christ. What an example this present passage is! The gospel was penetrating the "high places" of Rome, and into the stronghold of the imperial government. Praise the Lord! This is no time for discouragement and despair, but for rejoicing and praising God!

The words "greater progress" are based on two words. One, emphasizes a contrast to what they were thinking about Paul's circumstances. The word "greater" could be translated "rather," or "more." The sentence would read literally, "the things have come according to me *rather or more* unto progress of the gospel." This suggests that they were thinking the opposite. Surely now the Gospel would be hindered by Paul being in jail, they thought. But he wanted them to know that instead of hindering the work of the Gospel, his jail experience was increasing the opportunities for the Gospel's advancement.

The word "progress" is a combination of the verb "to cut" and the preposition "before." It was used of someone cutting a path through brush so others could follow. Paul was cutting a path for others to follow in terms of spreading the Gospel. The same word is used in verse 25 of chapter 1 and in I Timothy 4:15 of Timothy's progress in the Word so that others could follow.

B. The results of these circumstances — 1:13-14.

The words "so that" in verse 13 tell us some of the results that Paul was experiencing in spreading the Gospel at Rome. Two things are important to our study from these two verses. One deals with the *carrying* of Paul's testimony to everyone in that place.

> So that my imprisonment in the cause of Christ has become well-known
> throughout the whole praetorian guard and to everyone else (v. 13).

Not all of us can say that we have accomplished the purpose of God in the trying circumstances that we have faced in life. Paul speaks of the *display* of his "bonds" or his "imprisonment." He says it is "well-known," which means to be publicly displayed. He was not quiet in his witness in spite of the circumstances facing him. There is a time to be quiet and a time to speak. There is also the matter of the right time and appropriateness. But too often we simply do not speak the truth of the Gospel when we should!

The *description* of the ones who heard the Gospel—1:13—is truly amazing. The text reads literally, "in the whole Praetorium and to all the remaining ones." The Praetorium as used in the Gospels referred to the official residence in Jerusalem of the Roman governor. In Acts 23:35, the word refers to Herod's palace in Caesarea. It appears that the Praetorium was a typical name for the official government residence. It would be something like the "White House" in Washington, D.C. The only difference between the Praetoriums of the cities in Palestine and the one mentioned here is that this is the seat of the entire Roman empire—imperial Rome itself! The Gospel is now penetrating the heart of the empire! We are certain that the jury before whom Paul stood to give his "defense" was aware of his testimony, but how about the "whole Praetorium"? From chapter 4, verse 22, we realize that his testimony was so powerful that even members of Caesar's own family (Nero) became believers!

The second thing we see about the results of these circumstances is the *courage* which the believers developed through all of this.

> And that most of the brethren, trusting in the Lord because of my imprisonment, have far more courage to speak the word of God without fear (v. 14).

The word "most" tells us that not all believers felt this way. The *reason* why this courage developed in most lives is because these were "trusting in the Lord because of my imprisonment." God often brings trials to put us in the place of total dependence. He sometimes removes the people we were depending upon in order that we might depend solely upon Him.

It was and is the Lord who persuades our hearts. The immediate situation that stimulated this was the imprisonment of Paul. Where else could they turn but to the Lord? It seems that God delights in causing these problems in our lives that turn us in desperation to Him. The exciting thing is that He never gets tired of us saying, "help"! He wants us to come to Him. Hebrews 4:16 says "Let us therefore draw near with confidence to the throne of grace, that we may receive mercy and may find grace to help in time of need."

The *result* of this courage was that they were speaking the "word of God without fear." The root word translated "courage" means to "dare to do" something. Do it even when you know there are possible consequences. This boldness was because they were trusting in the Lord not in their own courage or abilities. The words "to speak" refer to a continual pattern or habit. They were continually speaking the word. And, of course, it was "without fear." When you're trusting in the Lord, there's nothing to be afraid of. II Timothy 1:7 says, "For God has not given us a spirit of timidity [fear] , but of power and love and discipline." Joshua was told (Joshua 1:9), "Have I not commanded you? Be strong and courageous! Do not tremble or be dismayed, for the Lord your God is with you wherever you go."

II. ACCEPTING YOUR CONFLICTS WITH OTHERS AS BEING FROM THE LORD AND FOR YOUR GOOD — 1:15-19

The second area in which our acceptance of difficult places is tested is in the area of conflicts with people. Somehow it seems easier to accept trying circumstances or events than it is to accept trying people! People who constantly rub you the wrong way. People with whom you do not get along. People who work overtime in hindering you as an individual in your life and work. It seems they delight in causing you problems. Now, how can a person have joy in the heart when he faces people like this? Again, our attention is centered on the personal example of Paul. Paul was aware of the motives and activities of certain people, but he didn't let it get to him. He recognized that God had permitted these people to affect his life, and he was learning to rejoice in God's wonderful plan.

In these verses there is the use of a construction in the original language (*men - de*) that carries the idea of the words "on the one hand . . . but, on the other hand." This construction is used twice in these verses to show the difference in attitude in two groups of people. The first difference centers on the *reason* for which they were preaching Christ (v. 15). The second difference centers on their *response* toward Paul (vv. 16-17).

The reason that is given for the group causing conflicts is described as "envy and strife." The word "envy" in verse 15 (*phthonon*) refers to the desire to deprive someone of what he has. It is malicious in motive. Some people did not like the leadership or authority of the Apostle Paul, and they were always trying to tear it down in the eyes of others. The word translated "strife" (*erin*) refers to "debate, contentions," or an "argumentative spirit." Some people thrive on that—always stirring up conflict and strife! And all of this in the name of preaching the Gospel of Christ! What is Paul's attitude? Strike back? Defend yourself? Give it to them? No! He says in verse 18, "Christ is proclaimed; and in this I rejoice, yes, and I will rejoice." What an attitude!

As to their response toward Paul personally, the one group who loved his leadership and his ministry responded "out of love" (v. 16) with the knowledge that he was facing trial and "defense of the Gospel." The other group who were questioning his authority and leadership responded "out of selfish ambition" (v. 17). The *problem* that was involved in their response was that it was not "from pure motives." It was characteristic of those who tried to win followers for themselves. Not only did this group want to deprive Paul of his leadership and ministry, but they also wanted to have people follow them! Such it is with many who are rebelling against leadership and authority. The old sin nature desires to have what another possesses (coveting).

The sinful *purpose* they had in all of this is expressed in the words of verse 17, "thinking to cause me distress in my imprisonment." That's what I call "hitting a man when he is down!" The word for "thinking" (*oiomenoi*) means "to expect or imagine." They were actually hoping that this would bring trouble to Paul. They figured that the more the Gospel was shared, the more upset the people of Rome would become and the less tolerant they would be of Paul. The word "cause" actually indicates that, for it is the common word "to raise up." They would be raising up "distress" or "affliction" for Paul in his imprisonment. It shows us the ends to which some people will go when they are filled with wrong motives and selfish ambition. Again, how should we respond to all of this? Rejoice! Christ is preached!

The great lesson we learn here is the rejoicing that Paul experienced in his heart. Verse 18 begins with the question, "What then?" (literally—"for what?"). Now what should be done? Paul answers with a rejoicing heart!

> Only that in every way, whether in pretense or in truth, Christ is proclaimed; and in this I rejoice, yes, and I will rejoice. For I know that this shall turn out for my deliverance through your prayers and the provision of the Spirit of Jesus Christ (vv. 18-19).

What a marvelous attitude! Rejoicing no matter what! His rejoicing appears to be based upon two things: One, the *preaching* or proclaiming of Christ; and two, the *prospect* of his deliverance. Paul states that "in every way" he rejoices when Christ is proclaimed. The word "way" is the word for "place." The point might be that in each place where Christ is proclaimed no matter what the motivation, he is happy—the Word is going out! The word "pretense" means "to appear before" and would indicate the motive was simply to be seen by others. The idea might also be that they were disguising their real motives. It appears by the statement "whether in pretense or in truth" that the issue here is motivation. "Truth" would emphasize the honesty of an individual. Whether merely a phony or being sincere, it did not matter to Paul. He rejoiced that Jesus Christ was preached. Undoubtedly many of the believers loyal to Paul were wondering what to do about this opposition and competition. Paul's answer: "Rejoice!"

His rejoicing was also based upon his prospect for deliverance. He states in verse 19, "For I know." This knowledge is usually based on facts that are available. He seemed confident because of the power of prayer and the provision of the Spirit of Jesus Christ. His *assurance* of deliverance is expressed in the words "this shall turn out for my deliverance." The word for "deliverance" is the word "salvation." It is used metaphorically here of events that will turn out for the better.

The *agency* through which Paul believed this deliverance would happen was twofold: One—their *prayers;* and, two, the *provision* of Christ's Spirit. The word "prayers" is the word meaning the expression of a need. Paul certainly had a need, and he felt confident that God would answer the prayers of His people. He also was basing this prospect of deliverance upon the provision of the Spirit of Jesus Christ. The word "provision" literally means "to lead a chorus" and also involved "defraying the expenses" in so doing. The word comes to mean "to supply fully." The Spirit always provides completely for our need. Paul's heart was centered on doing the will of God and preaching Christ whenever and to whomever he could. He had no worries. He knew that God would take care of him. He had the Spirit to rely upon to meet all his needs. He was confident in this case of being released soon.

III. ACCEPTING YOUR CHANCE TO EXALT JESUS CHRIST NO MATTER WHAT HAPPENS TO YOU — 1:20-21

In order to have joy in accepting difficult places that God puts you in, you will need to realize that this is your chance to exalt Jesus Christ. No matter what the situation in which you find yourself, it is an opportunity to give glory to God and exalt the name of Jesus Christ.

A. This chance to exalt Jesus was based upon Paul's expectation.

> According to my earnest expectation and hope, that I shall not be put
> to shame in anything, but that with all boldness, Christ shall even now,
> as always, be exalted in my body, whether by life or by death. For to
> me, to live is Christ, and to die is gain (1:20-21).

What tremendous words of commitment are expressed here! The words "expectation" and "hope" are equals. This means that you cannot divorce

Paul's expectation in the present situation from his hope. The word translated "expectation" (*apokaradokian*) means "watching with outstretched head." "From" emphasizing the turning away from anything that would detract you from that watching. It is an intense gazing upon something in the distance from you. It is an eager awaiting for it. The reference here is not to the second coming of Christ, although his desire to be with Christ by means of death was expressed in this section. His expectation deals with the exaltation of Jesus Christ! Imagine the commitment of this man under these circumstances! No matter what happened to him, his great desire was to exalt Jesus Christ! Is it so with us?

B. The <u>extent</u> of this commitment he had to Christ is expressed in about four ways in these two wonderful verses.

First, as to any personal *embarrassment,* he said, "in nothing I shall be ashamed." The word "ashamed" speaks of that which prevents a person from doing something. Often, believers shrink back from an opportunity to speak for Christ and exalt Him because of this kind of embarrassment. It holds us back from doing what we ought to do. Paul's commitment extended to this point—"in nothing" would he be embarrassed to speak of Jesus!

Second, as to the *expression* of his faith in the presence of others, he says, "with all boldness." The word "but" (*alla*) is a word of great contrast. In contrast to the embarrassment some would feel, Paul was committed to the principle of "boldness" which is also translated "freedom of speech." In Acts 4:31-33, we learn that boldness in speaking the word of God is the result of being filled with the Holy Spirit.

Third, as to the *exaltation* of Jesus Christ in everything, he says, "Christ shall even now, as always, be exalted in my body, whether by life or by death." The "now" would refer to the dire circumstances he was in. It made no difference to Paul! He was ready to preach Christ no matter what! The *means* used to accomplish this was his body." The "body" is simply a vehicle or instrument which God can use to express His life to a world that needs to know Him. Paul wrote of this frequently when he said, "Present your bodies" (Rom. 12:1) or "yield ye your [bodies] members" (Rom. 6:13) or "Your body is a temple of the Holy Spirit" (I Cor. 6:19), and so forth. The issue here is my hands to be His hands; my feet to be His feet; my mouth to be His mouth, and so on. It is God speaking and working through me. I am valuable to God. God wants to use me. Praise His name!

The *methods* by which this exaltation of Christ will be accomplished are often very different. "Whether by life or by death" are words which are easy to say, but difficult to accept at times. Who can say whether it is easier to live for Christ or to die for Him? Both are difficult. This commitment involves all of life, and if God wants to exalt Jesus by our physical death, then let it be so! We would be ushered into His presence immediately, for to be "absent from the body" is to be "present with the Lord!" (II Cor. 5:8).

Fourth, as to the *effects* upon Paul personally, he says, "For to me, to live is Christ, and to die is gain." This is our key verse to the philosophy of one who knows the joy of the Lord! To be living day after day is for one goal or purpose—Jesus Christ! The dying is gain because that's where we're headed! We'd just be going home! We're going to spend an eternity with Him! Stop laying up treasurers on earth—start laying them up in heaven! Be faithful unto death—there's a crown of victory awaiting us! No matter what happens in our lives, let's commit ourselves to Jesus Christ—to exalting Him in every situation! Then and only then will we be able to live "above the circumstances"!

STUDY QUESTIONS:

1. What reason did Paul give as to why he was in jail?

2. Why were some believers developing courage through Paul's imprisonment?

3. What were the motives of some people in preaching Christ but not caring what happened to Paul?

4. What was Paul's "expectation" and "hope"?

4 PHILIPPIANS 1:22-30

+++

Your Anticipation
of Christ's Presence

+++

THE CHAPTER OUTLINED:

   I. **The Necessity of Remaining Here on Earth**
      A. The productivity he could expect
      B. The pressure he felt
      C. The purpose he had
      D. The persuasion he had

  II. **The Need for Facing Opposition and Conflicts**
      A. As to your conduct
      B. As to the coming of Paul
      C. As to our commitment

SUGGESTED BACKGROUND DEVOTIONAL READING

Monday—Life Is Christ (Col. 3:1-4)

Tuesday—To Be with Him (I John 2:28—3:3)

Wednesday—He Is Coming (I Thess. 4:13-18)

Thursday—We Are Needed (Rom. 1:8-15)

Friday—Don't Be Ashamed (Rom. 1:16; 10:11-15)

Saturday—We Need Boldness (Acts 4:1-13)

Sunday—Called to Suffer (I Peter 2:18-25)

Paul's last statement in verse 21 is the natural transition to this next discussion dealing with the believer's anticipation of Christ's presence. Paul wrote in II Corinthians 5:8, "We are of good courage, I say, and prefer rather to be absent from the body and to be at home with the Lord." The discussion here is very practical in that it presents the dilemma of the believer who would like to go immediately to be with the Lord but who knows that God has a purpose for him in remaining here on earth. There are two basic lines of thought in these verses:

I. The necessity of remaining here on earth—1:22-26

II. The need for facing opposition and conflicts—1:27-30

Our anticipation of Christ's presence does not overlook or ignore the necessity of remaining here on earth in order to accomplish the tasks that God has given to us. Our Lord does not admonish us to sell all our possessions and depart to the top of a mountain and there await His return! His marching orders were, "Occupy till I come!" There's work to be done!

I. THE NECESSITY OF REMAINING HERE ON EARTH — Phil. 1:22-26

> But if I am to live on in the flesh, this will mean fruitful labor for me; and I do not know which to choose. But I am hard pressed from both directions, having the desire yet to depart and be with Christ, for that is very much better; yet to remain on in the flesh is more necessary for your sake. And convinced of this, I know that I shall remain and continue with you all for your progress and joy in the faith, so that your proud confidence in me may abound in Christ Jesus through my coming to you again.

A. The PRODUCTIVITY he could expect — 1:22.

Paul spoke of his labor on earth as being "fruitful." He was expecting that his service for Christ and his ministry in the lives of others would bear fruit. This "fruit" was definitely the result of work. We will never bear much fruit by just sitting around doing nothing! Whatever we sow, that we shall reap! We cannot violate the laws of the harvest in the spiritual realm anymore than in the physical realm. If we sow bountifully (II Cor. 9:6), we shall reap bountifully. This productivity was based upon three things:

1. It was based upon his *pattern of life* on earth—"But if I am to live on in the flesh." Literally, the text says, "But if the living (to be living— indicating a continual process or pattern of life) in flesh." He is speaking of his life on earth. The "if" would seem to suggest that he knew that this

was God's will for right now. It literally means: "If, and it is so," or "Since it is so." Paul does not seem doubtful at this point as to whether or not he would die. If he was, he could have used another word for "if." This matches with the overall situation in his life when he wrote Philippians. He was expecting to be released, and he knew that God had more work for him to do in the lives of others. The one thing we should learn from this is that the time to bear fruit is now! We should do all we can for Christ while we are still living! Our fruitfulness does not begin after we die or when we get to heaven. What you are going to do for Christ, you must do now while you still have time!

2. It was based upon the *principle* stated in verse 21. Verse 22 reads, "But if the living in flesh, *this* [is] to me fruit of work" (Lit. trans.). The word "this" refers to "the living in flesh" and reminds us of what verse 21 said: "For to me *the living* [is] Christ and the dying, gain" (Lit. trans.). "The living," or our life here on earth, will not be very productive unless we understand the overall motivation and driving force. It is Jesus Christ! The reason for living is Jesus! When we have our eyes fixed on Him, we can't help but be productive!

3. It was based upon the *problem* he faced—"and I do not know which to choose." The words "I do not know" come from a word meaning "to discover" or "to come to know." Paul had not yet discovered which thing he would choose over the other. This helps us to explain why he was so fruitful. To him, whether we live or die, Jesus Christ is the reason and motivation for both. The word "choose" means "to take for oneself." He did not see that one thing was better than the other. Both things were centered in the Person of Jesus Christ. Life on earth was Jesus—walking and working in the joy of His presence and love! To die was to be with Jesus—Praise the Lord! The real problem for many of us is the "on earth" thing. If we really don't enjoy the kind of life with Jesus—moment by moment—day by day—then we can't identify with Paul. Many of us would say, "I would choose heaven any day over what I have to go through down here!" And that, friends, is why we are often short on joy!

B. The PRESSURE he felt – 1:23.

The King James Version says, "I am in a strait betwixt two," and the New American Standard version says, "But I am hard pressed from both directions." The Greek text says "I am being held together out of the two." There seemed to be two things that were bringing this pressure upon him:

1. As to a *decision* between the two things. The two things involved staying here on earth to minister in the lives of others and going to be with the Lord. Paul said that he was "being held together" by these two things. You can interpret that as a difficult choice over which he was confused as to which was best, or as a simple fact that both of these things were having an affect upon his life. The first cannot be the point because he states that being with Christ would be far better. Naturally, it would be much better to see Christ physically than seeing Him with the eye of faith in the spiritual realm. The point seems to reflect back on verse 21. Whether Paul was living in the flesh on earth or whether he would die, his main motivation was Jesus Christ! So, both things "held him together."

2. As to his personal *desire*—"having the desire to depart and be with Christ, for that is very much better." The second thing that was bringing this pressure upon him was what he desired personally. He wanted to go home! The thing he was looking forward to was seeing Jesus, his Lord and Saviour! Are we anticipating that glorious day when we shall look upon His lovely face? To see Jesus will surely make everything we have endured and experienced down here "worth it all"!

a. The *means* by which this desire would be fulfilled is described in the words "to depart." The word means "to loose up" and suggests that it will come at any moment! The word was used in three basic ways in Roman-Greek times all of which are picturesque in describing the moment when we are caught up to meet the Lord in the air (I Thess. 4:16-17). First, it was used of "breaking camp." When the Roman armies moved their location they took up the stakes of their tents and moved on. We are just "pilgrims and strangers" in this world. Our "citizenship" is in heaven (Phil. 3:20). One day we will "pull up stakes" from our temporary earthly dwelling and take up permanent residence in eternity! Second, it is used of "setting sail." When the sailors got ready to leave a port or seashore, they pulled up the anchor and set sail. One day we shall leave the shore of this world and sail to another land! Third, it is used of taking the yoke off of animals. The trials and burdens (yoke) of this life will one day be completely removed, and we will "lay our burdens down."

b. The *motivation* behind all of this is "to be with Christ." So much could be said of this simple truth, but it is the kind of thing that one needs to meditate on rather than talk. To be with Christ—that is the real motivation for everything!

c. The *manner* in which it is described—"for that is very much better."

The Greek has three words: "much," "more," and "better." They may not be good English, but it is good Greek!

C. The PURPOSE he had – 1:24. – *minister & needs of others.*

In spite of Paul's personal desire to "be with Christ" which is obviously much better, he knew that God wanted him to stay here on earth for further ministry in the lives of people. He states that "to remain on in the flesh is more necessary for your sake." Paul was not thinking of himself when he made this remark. It was for "your sake." Literally it reads, "because of you." His basic reason centered in the needs of others rather than himself. The words "more necessary" simply emphasize "what needs be." It was not a necessity because Paul had a need in his life, but because this was God's plan for him and the Philippian believers had further need of his ministry.

D. The PERSUASION he had – 1:25-26.

There seems to be no doubt in Paul's mind that this was the will of God. We have already learned in this chapter about his conviction that he would be released. The phrase "and convinced of this" is in the perfect tense, meaning that he had already been persuaded of this and that conviction had not left him. The question might be, "How did Paul become persuaded of this?" Was it because of prayer or a direct revelation from God? Or, was it simply intuition? Or, perhaps the circumstances around his present imprisonment convinced him of this fact. What does the word "this" mean? It would seem to refer to what he stated in verse 24. Therefore, the meaning is that Paul had come to a persuasion that his ministry in their lives was still a necessity, and that on the basis of this, he felt confident that God would give him another opportunity to minister to them. This "persuasion" seems to affect three things.

1. As to his *presence* among them—in verse 25 he says, "I know that I shall remain and continue with you all." The second verb "continue" emphasizes the idea of remaining "alongside of" them. He was expecting to have a personal ministry with them again—in their presence! Quite a statement for a man who is in prison in Rome, Italy, and writing a letter to a city in Macedonia (northern Greece) in a day when travel was not the easiest thing in the world to do! The words "I know" indicates that he had some facts behind this persuasion of his.

2. As to their *progress* and joy of the faith—he believed that he would soon be ministering to them again because they had a need of progress in

their Christian faith. There seems to be an underlying need of the Philippian believers throughout this little book. Some writers would prefer to commend this church as one of the few without problems with the exception of a small incident mentioned in chapter 4, verse 2. However, through a continual reading of the book, one becomes aware that the church had a problem in maturity and in having the joy of the Lord. The word "progress" means "to cut before" (cf. Phil. 1:12). It appears in this verse that it is connected to the word "joy" in such a way as to indicate that both words are equal in thought. The "progress" they needed to make was in the area of "joy." The key problem, therefore, in the Book of Philippians is growing in joy. When the circumstances of life do not turn out the way we were counting on, we often lose our joy and become disappointed or bitter, failing to see the wonderful purposes of God in all of them. That is why Paul wrote this letter to the saints at Philippi. The "progress" in joy is also described as the "joy of the faith." The definite article "the" appearing before the word "faith" indicates the sum total of "the faith" for which we are to "earnestly contend" and which was "once for all delivered to the saints." It would refer to the Word of God, the message of faith. So, the growth they needed to experience was a growth in the Word, in the knowledge of God's will and plan, so that they would have the joy of the Lord at all times. How often in our own lives we fail to have the joy of the Lord because we have not been studying the Word! Psalm 16:11 reminds us, "In Thy presence is fulness of joy; in Thy right hand there are pleasures forever."

3. As to their *pride* in him—1:26—"so that your proud confidence in me may abound in Christ Jesus through my coming to you again." The words "proud confidence" are not emphasizing the idea of conceit as we would use the word "proud," but rather refer to the ground or basis of boasting or glorying. It can be used in a bad or good sense. It is not wrong to "boast" or "glory" in that which the Bible tells us is worthy of such commendation. Certainly we are to "boast in the Lord," and in certain things we also are to "boast" in others in whom the Lord is working and blessing. The "boasting" they had in Paul was based on the ministry he had in their lives and on that basis, was proper and good. Let's look at two things affecting this "pride" in Paul.

a. The *manner* in which that pride should be expressed—verse 26 states "may abound in Christ Jesus." The sphere in which this "pride" or "boasting" should be increased is the Person of Jesus Christ. When we see what

God is doing through some person, we should praise the Lord! I Corinthians 1:31 says: "Let him who boasts, boast in the Lord." Paul was careful to put the emphasis where it belonged—"in Christ Jesus." *boast in Lord*

b. The *means* by which this would be accomplished—"through my coming to you again." The word "coming" is the word emphasizing "presence" or "arrival." The word "again" reminds us that Paul's previous ministry among them brought joy to their hearts and was a ministry for which they were praising the Lord. Paul now indicates that he wants his presence with them again to bring joy and boasting that will abound in the Lord.

These verses (Phil. 1:22-26) have stressed one great truth in the life of Paul from which we can learn. In our anticipation of Christ's presence we must remember that it is often necessary that we remain on earth to minister to others. Some of us are ready to go to heaven just to escape the pressures and problems of this earth. We can know the joy of His presence now! It is necessary for us to remain here (if you are still here!) or God would have already taken us home!

II. THE NEED FOR FACING OPPOSITION AND CONFLICTS—1:27-30

> Only conduct yourselves in a manner worthy of the gospel of Christ; so that whether I come and see you or remain absent, I may hear of you that you are standing firm in one spirit, with one mind striving together for the faith of the gospel; in no way alarmed by your opponents—which is a sign of destruction for them, but of salvation for you, and that too, from God. For to you it has been granted for Christ's sake, not only to believe in Him, but also to suffer for His sake, experiencing the same conflict which you saw in me, and now hear to be in me.

If we shall remain on earth to perform a ministry in the lives of others, we must face the fact that we will face opposition and conflict at one time or another. Verse 27 begins by placing the word "only" (*monon*) in the emphatic position. The emphasis is upon the real need in the light of what was just said in the preceding verses. It deals with the kind of conduct we should have as we remain here on earth to minister to others.

A. As to your CONDUCT – 1:27.

Paul said, "Only conduct yourselves in a manner worthy of the gospel of Christ. . . ."

1. The *meaning* of the word "conduct" (*politeuesthe*). Our word "political" comes from this Greek word. It refers to the matter of being a good

citizen or conducting yourself appropriately. A form of the word appears in chapter 3, verse 20, where it states that our "citizenship is in heaven." It is commanded here by Paul.

2. The *manner* in which we are to be a citizen. The words "in a manner worthy of" come from a word meaning a "balance" or "having the weight of" something. In the bartering system of the ancient world, a system of balances was used to determine the value of some item. In Ephesians 4:1 it says, "I therefore, the prisoner of the Lord, entreat you to walk in *a manner worthy of* the calling with which you have been called." The same word (*axios*) appears in that verse. The idea is to make sure your conduct matches with the content of what you say you believe. In simple words—"practice what you preach!"

3. The *motivation* of this conduct—"the gospel of Christ." We are to conduct ourselves in a manner worthy of, or balanced with, the Gospel of Christ. From what Paul states in verses 28-30, it appears that he is referring to our attitude toward suffering, and especially the suffering that we experience at the hands of those who oppose the Gospel (v. 28). The Messiah taught that we should love our enemies and do good to those who hate us. Paul certainly reflected a proper attitude in the earlier section of this chapter in verses 15-18. This "Gospel" is not only the one the Messiah gave and taught, but also the Gospel about the Messiah and His life. I Peter 2:21-23 reminds us of His great example:

> For you have been called for this purpose, since Christ also suffered for you, leaving you an example for you to follow in His steps, who committed no sin, nor was any deceit found in His mouth; and while being reviled, He did not revile in return; while suffering, He uttered no threats, but kept entrusting Himself to Him who judges righteously.

B. As to the COMING of Paul – 1:27.

Paul wrote, ". . . so that whether I come and see you or remain absent, I may hear of you. . . ." Paul certainly expected to visit them in the near future (vv. 24-25). However, whether he did or not, they needed to go on in their spiritual development and progress, regardless of his presence. It would be easier for them to face conflicts and opposition as long as Paul, the veteran warrior, was there. We will not always have the support of those who have been our spiritual leaders. There is a time when we must take the leadership and begin to trust God to give us courage and wisdom in difficult situations.

C. As to our COMMITMENT — 1:27-30.

The remaining verses of this chapter are emphasizing the commitment that all of us need when facing conflicts and opposition to our message and our way of life.

1. The main *requirement*—"... that you are standing firm in one spirit...." The word for "standing" could be a simple statement of fact—"you are standing" or a command—"stand." The King James takes the view that it is a statement of fact—"that ye stand in one spirit." The New American Standard Bible takes that view and also holds that it is a present tense—"you are standing." Paul said: "I may hear of you that you are standing." It would seem a little strange for him to say that statement as a command since he is only hearing of the fact. Certainly, if Paul had been in their midst he might have given this as a command. He wanted to hear that it was a fact which characterized their conduct or manner of life. He felt that it was the great need in the light of conflicts and opposition which they must face. "To stand" suggests that we ought not to move our position. It suggests resistance to something as well. The context shows us that there was real opposition to face.

2. The two *results* of this requirement. The first one is found in the phrase "with one mind striving together for the faith of the gospel."

a. As to *contending* for the faith of the Gospel. The word "striving together" combines the preposition "with" (*sun*) and the word for "athlete" (*athlountes*). This word refers to contending in games or could be translated as "contest." The word is again used by Paul in chapter 4, verse 3, where it is translated "shared my struggle." The way in which we are to contend for the faith of the Gospel is "with one mind" which literally is "with one soul." When Paul referred to their standing firm he used the phrase "in one spirit." Here he expands on that idea with the words "with one soul." James 1:8 tells us "a double-minded man [is] unstable in all his ways." The word "double-minded" is "two souled" (*dipsuchos*). When your heart or your mind is going in two different directions it produces an unstable life. This word is often used to refer to different motivations or ulterior motives. The point in Philippians 1:27 would be a single-mindedness. It's like saying "put your heart and soul into it!" The believers needed to be together in this matter of contending for the faith of the Gospel and their heart needed to be in it.

b. As to *courage* when facing your opposition—"in no way alarmed by your opponents." The word "alarmed" simply means "to scare." Literally, the text says, "not being scared in anything." Not one thing should frighten us! II Timothy 1:7 says, "For God has not given us a spirit of timidity, but of power and love and discipline." This is really describing what it is to be "standing firm." The source of possible fear is described as "your opponents." The word means "to set against" or "to lie opposite to" and would refer to the nonbeliever who is constantly opposing what the believer is and stands for. There is plenty of that kind of opposition in our world today just as there was in Paul's day. Jesus told us that if the world hated Him we could count on it hating us. Thus, we need to "stand firm"! This involves both contending (athletic contest) for the faith of the Gospel as well as having courage when facing the opposition.

3. The *response* you can expect—1:28—". . . which is a sign of destruction for them, but of salvation for you, and that too, from God." This response is divided up between "them" and "you."

a. *To them*—it is a sign of destruction! The word "sign" means "a pointing out" or "showing forth." The word "evidence" or "proof" would be a good translation. Their opposition is all the proof you need of their final end—"destruction." However, the point here seems to be that they regard your courage against their opposition as a waste of time or a complete loss. It is "evidence" which is *"to them"* or in their eyes. The word "destruction" means "waste, ruin, or loss."

b. *For you*—it is evidence of salvation! We know that we are really saved when we manifest such courage in the face of opposition! Also, when we face that opposition we see how really important it is to believe what we believe! What encouragement to those who are facing opposition from nonbelievers! It is "evidence" or "proof" of our salvation! After all, if you were a nonbeliever, you would not experience that kind of opposition! Paul tells them also that the real source of this courage and encouragement is God Himself—"and that too, from God." What a comfort in the midst of testing and conflicts to know that it is "from God"!

4. The *realization* of suffering—1:29-30. Verse 29 begins with the word "for," (*hoti*) which means "because." Here we learn of the cause and reason for all of this conflict and opposition that we must face.

a. The *source* of this suffering—"For to you it has been granted for Christ's sake." The word "granted" is the word for "grace" (*echaristhe*) and we could translate, "because to you it was graced." It was "in behalf of Christ" that we have been given the privilege of suffering in this way. The one who "graced" or gave this to us would be God the Father. The motivation was in behalf of His Son, Jesus Christ. It is not because God wants to punish us or make things difficult for us that He allows us to experience suffering and conflict. It is truly a result of His "grace." It is the very thing we need to build our lives and to get us positive evidence of our conversion or our relationship to Him. I Peter 5:10 tells us, "And after you have suffered for a little, the God of all *grace,* who called you to His eternal glory in Christ, will Himself perfect, confirm, strengthen, and establish you."

b. The *start* of this suffering—"not only to believe in Him." The point at which this suffering was graced or given to us is the believing into Him. This message needs to be made clear to the new convert. Too often our message implies that to receive Christ is to remove all difficulty, hardship, and problems from the believer. We all know that this is not the case. Much suffering will come to us and in various ways and forms. God is using all of it to build us to maturity and to give us a more effective ministry in the lives of others, and also to cause us to concentrate on eternal values.

c. The *substance* of this suffering—"but also to suffer for His sake." The word for "suffering" is used 42 times in the New Testament with most of its usages referring to the death and crucifixion of Jesus Christ. It was truly the hour of "suffering"! He suffered much for us. The suffering we do for Him is in some respect similar to His. He suffered the opposition, hostility, and sinfulness of those who despised and rejected Him. We also, according to this passage, are suffering in His behalf when we stand up to the opposition and conflict which nonbelievers bring to us.

d. The *similarity* of this suffering to Paul's own experience. Verse 30 says, "experiencing the same conflict which you saw in me, and now hear to be in me." The word "conflict" is our word "agony." "Experiencing" is the simple word "having." Paul refers to the fact that they were having the same kind of agony over various conflicts and opposition that they originally saw in him when he was at Philippi the first time, and which they were now hearing about him through his imprisonment in Rome. Thus, Paul's letter was written to encourage these young believers in difficult times, and to show them the principles of joy.

The first section of our study in Philippians is entitled, "THE PHILOSOPHY OF YOUR LIFE MUST BE CENTERED IN JESUS CHRIST." We have shown that this involves three basic things:

1. Your attitudes toward other people—1:1-11

2. Your acceptance of difficult places—1:12-21

3. Your anticipation of Christ's presence—1:22-30

None of us will have a full and complete joy if we are deficient in any of these areas. We often have wrong attitudes toward people instead of praising God for them and praying for them. We frequently rebel over the difficult situations into which God has placed us, instead of seeing them as real opportunities to witness for Him. And, most importantly, we often fail to keep our eyes on the right thing—namely, JESUS! We are not anticipating His presence. The joy of the Christian experience is Jesus—being with Him!

STUDY QUESTIONS:

1. What was the major dilemma which Paul described he had in his life?

2. What was the reason why Paul felt he needed to remain in the flesh?

3. In what two ways is the term "standing firm" described in these verses?

4. In what way do we suffer as Jesus suffered?

5. How are we usually affected when we face opposition from the nonbelieving world?

Principles of Joy

+++

PRINCIPLE NO. 2

THE PATTERN OF YOUR LIFE MUST BE CONFORMED TO JESUS CHRIST

Philippians 2:1-30

KEY VERSE: Philippians 2:5—"Have this attitude in yourselves which was also in Christ Jesus."

CHAPTER FIVE
YOUR ACKNOWLEDGMENT OF CHRIST'S PERSON
Philippians 2:1-11

CHAPTER SIX
YOUR APPLICATION OF GOD'S PURPOSES
Philippians 2:12-18

CHAPTER SEVEN
YOUR APPRECIATION OF GOD'S PEOPLE
Philippians 2:19-30

5 PHILIPPIANS 2:1-11

+++

Your Acknowledgment of Christ's Person

+++

THE CHAPTER OUTLINED:

   I. **The Exhortation That Is Involved**
      A. The basis of this exhortation
      B. The benefits of this exhortation

  II. **The Example of His Life**
      A. The command to us
      B. The characteristics of His life
      C. The experience of His death
      D. The exaltation of His name

SUGGESTED BACKGROUND DEVOTIONAL READING

Monday—The Danger of Disunity (James 3:13-18)

Tuesday—The Source of Strife (James 4:1-10)

Wednesday—The Unity of the Spirit (Eph. 4:1-6)

Thursday—Incarnation of Christ (John 1:1-14)

Friday—Equal with God (John 5:5-18)

Saturday—Christ the Servant (Matt. 20:20-28)

Sunday—The Exalted Christ (Heb. 1:1-4)

The second principle of joy from this little book that we want to study is that *the pattern of your life must be conformed to Jesus Christ.* The key verse states it well in Philippians 2:5: "Have this attitude in yourselves which was also in Christ Jesus." The opening part of chapter 2 will center our attention upon our Lord Jesus Christ. Having joy in your life certainly comes from knowing Jesus Christ! The more we learn of Him, the greater our joy! We will be looking at the following four things:

I.   The exhortation that is involved — 2:1-4
II. The example of His life — 2:5-8
III. The experience of His death — 2:8
IV. The exaltation of His name — 2:9-11

The exhortation that begins this chapter of Philippians is based upon the Person of Jesus Christ. The basic thought centers around the unity of believers and how that should be manifested in our daily attitudes toward one another.

I. THE EXHORTATION THAT IS INVOLVED — 2:1-4

The word "therefore" in verse 1 reminds us of the context preceding it. In the light of the sufferings of Christ and the prospect that we will suffer also, there is a need for attitudes of love and unity among the believers. We need to mutually encourage one another. Paul has just demonstrated in the last half of the first chapter that he felt it was necessary for him to remain in the flesh in order to minister to them. He was giving an example to them of the proper attitudes. In spite of the serious circumstances in which he found himself in that Roman prison, he was more interested in the welfare and spiritual growth of others. In this, he had the "mind of Christ."

A. The BASIS of this exhortation — 2:1

There are four different ways to interpret the word "if," which in Greek will be clearly indicated by the word used and the moods of the verbs used. In this passage the meaning is "if, and it is true!" You could translate "since it is true." The four things that follow are statements of fact which are true in the life of the believer.

1. The *consolation* in Christ—"If therefore there is any encouragement in Christ." The word translated "encouragement" (*paraklesis*) means "one called alongside of." It is the word used to describe the Holy Spirit (and Jesus) as the "Comforter." In the King James Version you will see this

word translated "consolation" (example—II Cor. 1:3-7) and also "comfort." The word "encouragement" is often used and is a good one, and sometimes you'll find the word "exhortation," which often confuses the modern reader. We think of exhortation as really strong rebuke or "giving it to them!" This word refers to the person-to-person counsel and encouragement that one receives. It is always upbuilding to a person's life. The point is that there *is* encouragement in the Person of Jesus Christ; and since there is, let's minister to the needs of one another and be more concerned about them than ourselves.

2. The *comfort* of love—"if there is any consolation of love." The word translated "consolation" combines the word for "speech" (*muthos*) and the word for "alongside of" (*para*). The meaning, therefore, is "a speaking closely to anyone." This word seems to have a greater degree of tenderness than the first word used—"encouragement." It is described as the "comfort of love." It is love that produces this kind of comfort in an hour of trial.

3. The *companionship* of the Spirit—"if there is any fellowship of the Spirit." The word "fellowship" (*koinonia*) refers to that which we share in common. Here it is described as the "fellowship of spirit." There is no definite article before the word "spirit," and thus, you could have two possible interpretations. One would be that the word "spirit" would refer to the disposition of the believer or his heart attitude, or mental response; the second would refer this to the Holy Spirit. It would seem that this latter view is the best one. The basis of urging these believers to unity and love would be the fact of their sharing the common life of God's Holy Spirit in them.

4. The *compassion* of Christ for us—"if any affection and compassion." Two words are used here to describe one basic idea of compassion. The first word refers to the "bowels" as physical organs or the "intestines." The Greeks would use this to illustrate deep affection. The second word is the word for "mercies." It carries the idea of "pity." It is used of God in II Corinthians 1:3 when it describes Him as the "Father of mercies," and also in Romans 12:1 when it says, "I urge you therefore, brethren, by the mercies of God." The word refers to God's deep concern for us which is so often manifested in what He does for us. Since there is this compassion, the point is, let's use it toward one another!

B. The BENEFITS of this exhortation — 2:2-4.

1. As to the *achieving* of a fulfilled joy—2:2. Paul says, "make my joy

complete." It is commanded on the basis of what he said in verse 1. Since these things of verse 1 really exist in the life of the believer, they will produce a unity among all the believers that makes the joy of becoming a believer more complete as well as the joy of the one who was instrumental in introducing you to Christ! Paul had "joy" over his first visit to Philippi as many received the Lord. His emphasis here is on their continued growth and maturity. His joy would be more complete if they would have unity and manifest a spirit of love and encouragement toward one another. It appears on the basis of what he says in these verses that this church might have been having a problem of disunity and lack of care and compassion among the believers. Philippians 4:2 would seem to indicate that this was so between two people at least. The problem might have been more extensive, and thus, the reason for dealing with it in these verses. The two problems of the Philippian believers seem to be unity and joy.

    2. As to their *association* with one another—2:2. The word "by" in verse 2 is a word of purpose, meaning, "in order that." This would explain how Paul's joy would be made complete and the purpose behind his remarks in this passage. The last phrase of this verse repeats the first thought, and is not a separate idea, but emphasizes the main point. In English, the New American Standard Bible says "by being of the same mind, maintaining the same love, united in spirit, intent on one purpose." The last phrase, "intent on one purpose," means "minding the one [thing]." The first phrase, "being of the same mind," means "you mind the same [thing]." The first phrase is the central point and the next three phrases merely expand on the meaning of it. To put it simply, Paul is here stressing a mental and spiritual unity among the believers upon the basis of what he said in verse 1. In their association with one another, they need to understand the importance of unity.

    a. There is to be a unity in *ministry* to one another—"maintaining the same love." Literally, it says, "having [continuously] the same love." There ought to be a continuous love among the believers for one another.

    b. There is to be a unity in *motives*—"united in spirit," which means "souls together." What a beautiful expression! James 1:8 speaks of a "double-minded" man, which means "two-souls." The point being ulterior motives, or different directions in the inner man, the soul. To have our souls together indicates a real unity and common purpose. Our motivations will be the same.

    c. There is to be a unity in *mind*—"intent on one purpose" or as we said earlier, "minding the one [thing] ." It is difficult to have an actual unity when we are not thinking alike or concentrating on the same things. When this is so, our unity is only theory, and not practice.

3. As to their *attitudes* toward one another—2:3-4. This section is extremely practical and detailed. We are not left "up in the air" as to what is involved in the matter of unity and how it would be accomplished. The basic problem here centers around the way we look at each other and the regard we have for what others think and do. We are all so self-centered! These attitudes involve two basic things:

a. The *importance* of the other person—2:3—"Do nothing from selfishness or empty conceit, but with humility of mind let each of you regard one another as more important than himself." Negatively, we are told to do "nothing from selfishness or empty conceit." The word for "selfishness" (*eritheian*) refers to selfish ambition. It is the spirit of one who wants his own way. He is motivated by a desire for personal gain or popularity, and cares little about whom he hurts in getting it! The words "empty conceit" come from two words: one, is the word for "empty" or "nothing to it"; the other, from the word "glory." When one is sought to bring glory to himself, it is an empty glory! It is a big waste of time!

Positively, we are told with humility of mind let each of you regard one another as more important than himself." "Humility of mind" refers to "lowliness." The same thought is expressed in Ephesians 4:2—"with all humility." Verse 3 of that chapter says, "being diligent to preserve the unity of the Spirit in the bond of peace." In other words, it is difficult to have real unity among the believers when humility is not present. The specific attitude of humility that is urged upon the Philippian believers is regarding others as more important than yourself. The word translated "regard" means "to lead." The idea is to "lead before the mind" or to "consider." The words "more important" mean "holding above" or "being superior." In lowliness of mind we are to continually consider others as more significant and important than ourselves. One can only do this when he reflects back to the basis of this exhortation found in verse 1. When we look at Jesus, then we get a proper perspective!

b. The *interests* of the other person—2:4—"do not merely look out for your own personal interests, but also for the interests of others." The second thing that is involved in our attitudes toward one another is not only regarding others as more important, but looking out for their interests rather than our own. The word to "look out" refers to mental consideration. Our English word "scope" comes from this word. The word for "bishop" (*episkopos*) is based on this word also. A bishop is one who "looks upon" those over whom he has responsibility, caring for their interests and needs. The word "others" (*heteron*) refers to others of a different kind, rather than others of the same kind. The point is that not everyone will have the same interests. It is real love when we show concern for the interests of someone else when those interests are not the same as the ones we have. We always want to talk about the things that interest us and concern us, rather than being concerned about what someone else likes or needs.

These first four verses seem to indicate that a problem did exist among the Philippian believers, and it is obvious that it is a common problem among all believers. Churches frequently experience a lack of unity and love among their people. It can happen between two people, a small group, or an entire congregation. The root always seems to lie in the selfishness of people; when we think of ourselves first, rather than others. These verses exhort us to unity! This unity must be in mental attitude as well as in actual practice. The way we think reveals the way we are and what we will eventually do. If we think properly, we will usually act properly. In order for us to see how this unity and humility among the believers can operate, Paul will now take us into the depths of Christ's own life, examining His example, and challenging us to have His "mind" in us! The key verse of this whole chapter and of our second principle of joy is verse 5—"Have this attitude in yourselves which was also in Christ Jesus." It is a mistake to look at others as our example unless they are following the example of Christ. We need to see Jesus!

II. THE EXAMPLE OF HIS LIFE – 2:5-8

We have before us now one of the greatest passages in all the Bible dealing with the Person of our Lord and Saviour Jesus Christ. It deals with the problem of His deity and humanity as they operated and existed in one person.

> Have this attitude in yourselves which was also in Christ Jesus, who, although He existed in the form of God, did not regard equality with God a thing to be grasped, but emptied Himself, taking the form of a bond-servant, and being made in the likeness of men. And being found in appearance as a man, He humbled Himself . . . (Phil. 2:5-8).

A. The COMMAND to us – 2:5.

"Have this attitude in yourselves which was also in Christ Jesus." The words "have this attitude" come from the same word used in verse 2–"mind"; "be mindful of." It refers to moral interest or reflection, and not a mere opinion. The thing which we are to be mindful of is "that which is in Christ Jesus" and this is the basis behind what Paul said in verse 2. The unity that is needed among believers will come as we look at the Person of Christ and examine the quality of His life. It is commanded of us and implies a constant reflection and study.

B. The CHARACTERISTICS of His life which are to be a part of us – 2:6-8.

Verse 6 begins with the relative pronoun "who" and refers to Jesus Christ. It is an expansion on "that which is in Jesus Christ." One almost feels as if he should take off his shoes, as Moses did long ago, because the place where he is standing is "holy ground."

1. As to His true *identity*–2:6. "Who, although He existed in the form of God, did not regard equality with God a thing to be grasped."

a. The *revelation* of this identity. It is revealed to us by two statements in this one verse:

(1) "Being in the form of God." The word "being" means "to exist." The idea is that He has always existed and is existing in that form at the present moment. It is a statement to His preexistence. The fact being referred to in these verses is the incarnation of Christ. This existence being mentioned in this verse is a state prior to the fact of the incarnation. At the point He "emptied Himself," He was already "existing in the form of God." Therefore, Jesus Christ existed before He was born as a babe in Bethlehem! He said in John 8:58, "Truly, truly, I say to you, before Abraham was born, I AM." The Jews of His day were not mistaken about this claim because the next verse says, "Therefore they picked up stones to throw at Him; but Jesus hid Himself, and went out of the temple." They knew that He was claiming to be God!

The words "form of God" (*morphe theou*) are oustanding testimony to the deity of Jesus Christ! The word "form" (*morphe*) refers to the essence, nature, or substance of a thing that is seen. It is an external form which is indicative of an internal nature or substance. It is reality in manifestation. No stronger word could be used to affirm the deity of our Lord and Saviour Jesus Christ. He is God in very essence, substance, and being. John 1:1 states, "In the beginning was the Word, and the Word was with God, and the Word was God." That last phrase affirms that Jesus Christ is God! The word "God" is in the emphatic position in that phrase, making it read, "and God was the Word!" The absence of the definite article "the" before God greatly emphasizes that the "Word" was God in essence, substance, and being. The absence of the article emphasizes the quality and substance of it. Make no mistake about it! Jesus is the eternal God in human form!

(2) "Equal to God." Although Jesus was existing in the form of God at the point of His incarnation, He did not think it a thing to be grasped or seized that He was "equal with God." The point here is that this verse states He was "equal to God." The word "equal" comes from a root (*isos*) meaning the same in size, number or quality. This would denote the various states in which the nature of deity could exist.

b. His *response* to His true identity—"did not regard equality with God a thing to be grasped." The word for "grasped" means "to seize; carry off by force." It was used of robbers who plunder and steal. This is quite a contrast to Satan who once counted being on equality with God a thing to be grasped as a robber might grasp (Isa. 14). Equality with God was so truly Christ's own possession that without the slightest bit of anxiety, He laid it aside for our sakes. And He did not feel as Satan did that it was a thing to be seized and grasped or even paraded before men. In the days of His flesh He was still equal with God and still in the form of God, and there is much in the Gospels to remind us of that fact.

2. As to His *incarnation*—2:7—"but emptied Himself, taking the form of a bond-servant, and being made in the likeness of men."

a. The *meaning* of "emptied." The central thought of this passage is centered in the meaning of the word "emptied" (*ekenosen*). Of what did our Lord empty Himself when He came into the world? Tremendous controversies have raged in church history over the meaning of this word. Some teach that He emptied Himself of His divine nature. Others say that He laid aside His divine attributes. Some say that He laid aside the exercise of His divine attributes and power. Yet, all of these ideas are inadequate. Christ certainly declared His own deity while here on the earth, and He certainly exercised divine power and manifested divine attributes! The simplest answer to this question is found in the text itself. He "emptied *Himself*." It is a self-emptying that becomes our example in our relationships with one another. The way this was done is described in the next phrase.

b. The *manner* in which this occurred—"taking the form of a bond-servant." The word "taking" could be translated "after taking" or "when taking." To be strict, it seems that this "taking" would precede the word "emptied" from the standpoint of time. Christ did this Himself. He made the decision! He became the perfect bond servant of the Father. He willingly subordinated Himself to the will of the Father. He was the only absolutely perfect bond servant! In John 5:19 Jesus said, "Truly, truly, I say to you, the Son can do nothing of Himself, unless it is something He sees the Father doing; for whatever the Father does, these things the Son also does in like manner." In John 12:49-50 Jesus said, "For I did not speak on My own initiative, but the Father Himself who sent Me has given Me commandment, what to say, and what to speak. And I know that His commandment is eternal life; therefore the things I speak, I speak just as the Father has told Me." The Father's will was the will of the Son, and these two were so uniquely blended together that Jesus could say in John 10:38—"the Father is in Me, and I in the Father," or in John 10:30, "I and the Father are one," or in John 14:9, "He who has seen Me has seen the Father."

The word "form" in verse 7 is the same word used in verse 6 when it says the "form of God." The meaning is that the true nature of Christ was that of a bond servant. The outward manifestation was indicative of the true internal reality—He was a bond servant, completely submissive to the will of His Father! The "emptying" of Christ was a voluntary decision on His part that was possible only because He was the perfect bond servant, fully able to submit Himself totally to the will of His Father. Only God could have done that! The "emptying" of Christ is not showing His fallibility while here on earth, but rather teaches His infallibility when He speaks! He could not make a mistake; He could do no wrong!

The last phrase of verse 7 says, "and being made in the likeness of men." It is another description of what it means when Christ "emptied Himself." There was a change of condition. He "became flesh." John 1:14—"the Word became flesh" (same Greek word used). The word "likeness" emphasizes that which is made like something, meaning a "resemblance." He was not merely a man, but He was man! He looked like a man, and that change of His previous preexistent state was a greaty "emptying." He condescended to the level of humanity!

3. As to His *identification* with human life—2:7-8—". . . and being made in the likeness of men. And being found in appearance as a man, He humbled Himself . . . ."

a. The *nature* of this identification—2:7. The words "being found" can also be translated "to discover" or "to learn." The emphasis here would be on His knowing human life by personal experience. The word "appearance" emphasizes the outward appearance as other men saw Him. He was definitely recognized as a man and functioned and performed as a man would in every respect except one—He was sinless!

b. The *need* for a change in His previous state in order to accomplish this—2:8—"He humbled Himself." The word "humbled" means "to make low." One can't help but remember the words in verse 3, "with humility of mind" or "lowliness of mind." The same root word is used there. Paul is using the example of Christ to teach us concerning our attitudes toward one another. This word "humbled" indicates that it was a great descent from His original position to His identification with man. The word "Himself" indicates that it was voluntary. He was willing to do it. One of the great treasures which this writer has in his library is a copy of the actual notes used by Dr. Alva J. McClain when he preached a series of sermons on Philippians in the fall of 1920. The notebook in which they are contained is well worn and now showing its age. It is such a joy to read the comments (well preserved and quite thorough even in note form!) of this great man of God now gone home to be with His Lord whom he loved so much! One section of those notes which is invaluable deals with the statement, "He humbled Himself." The words are reproduced here just like they appear in those notes.

> As God, He emptied Himself and took upon Himself the form of a servant—as man. He humbled Himself and became obedient unto death. From God, He stooped to humanity; from humanity, He stooped to death. A striking thought! The voluntariness of the Son of God! He came to earth to be one with us. To die for us—not from external compulsion nor from pressure brought to bear, but of Himself, voluntarily, of His own free will! He was limited only in His choice by His own loving, holy will. He emptied *Himself*; He humbled *Himself*! Never forget, on the other hand, that our blessed Lord was acting as a sovereign, in obedience to the Father's will. "Humbled Himself and became obedient unto death" does not mean for a moment that He became obedient to *death.* Death had no claim on the Son of God! He became obedient unto His Father, whose bond servant He was. He obeyed God so utterly, so completely as to be willing to die—not obeying death, but He was obeying the Father *unto* death. In the death of the cross, there was the marvelous blending of sovereign choice and utter obedience.

To this we would say "Amen!" It remains a mystery to us as to how the eternal God could have done this! But praise God, He did!

C. The EXPERIENCE of His death — 2:8.

". . . becoming obedient to the point of death, even death on a cross."

1. It was based on His *submission* to the Father's will—"becoming obedient." The word "becoming" means this obedience happened in a moment of time. Jesus made the decision immediately—no hesitation here, nor continual process of evaluation. He willingly and decisively was obedient to the Father's will. What a tremendous example for us! The word "obedient" comes from the word "to hear" or "to listen" plus the preposition "under." To "listen under" indicates an obedient response to another's authority. In Ephesians 6:1 the same word is used when it tells children to "obey" their parents.

2. It was based on the *salvation* He would provide—"to the point of death, even death on a cross." Christ came into the world to die! It was God's plan and will. It was no accident that He died on that cross. It was not a thwarting of God's plan or an interruption that was not expected! Jesus constantly told His disciples that He was going to die! The heart of the Gospel of our salvation is that Christ "died for our sins." It is "through His blood" that we have forgiveness of our sins. Christ willingly became obedient to the death of a cross because He was providing salvation for us—praise His wonderful name! At that moment on the cross He bore our sins, and we see the depth of meaning in the words, "He humbled Himself." Here was the eternal God in human flesh, dying on a cruel cross in deep humiliation—and why? Because He loved and loves us! What grace is this! What love!

D. The EXALTATION of His name — 2:9-11.

> Therefore also God highly exalted Him, and bestowed on Him the name which is above every name, that at the name of Jesus every knee should bow, of those who are in heaven, and on earth, and under the earth, and that every tongue should confess that Jesus Christ is Lord, to the glory of God the Father.

The first word in verse 9 is the word "therefore." In the light of His becoming man and dying on the cross, here's what God the Father has done! It would read "because of which thing." The "thing" referred to would be specifically the death on a cross. It's because of that cross that God had exalted Him.

1. The *source* of this exaltation—"God highly exalted Him." The reference is, of course, to the Father. The words "highly exalted" mean "to lift up over." Interestingly, the root verb "to lift up" is used of the cross of

Christ in John 3:14; 8:28; and 12:32, 34. Not only was Christ lifted up on that cross, but now the Father has lifted Him up above every thing!

2. The *scōpe* of this exaltation—"and bestowed on Him the name which is above every name." The word "bestowed" (*echarisato*) is the word for "grace." The Father "graced" this name to the Son. The name is above (*huper*) every name! The meaning is that His name is more important and greater in position and authority than any other name on earth!

a. As to its *motive* towards Christ. The little word "that" in verse 10 is a word of purpose. Here is the motive behind this exaltation.

(1) *Submission by all creation*—"that at the name of Jesus every knee should bow, of those who are in heaven, and on earth, and under the earth." Those in heaven would refer to all the angelic creatures; those on earth, to human beings; and those under the earth, to fallen angels or demons, or possibly to those dead or more specifically, the wicked dead. There is some disagreement as to the meaning of the phrase "under the earth." The word in Greek (*katachthonion*) combines the word for "deep" or "ground" with the preposition "down." "Down deep" is a good translation. The point is that all creation will bow the knee before Christ and recognize His greatness and Person! This includes all unbelievers as well who must stand before Him as their Judge!

(2) *Confession that He is Lord*—"and that every tongue should confess that Jesus Christ is Lord." To confess is to agree or acknowledge the same thing as God does. All people, believers and unbelievers, will confess that He is Lord! The question is not, "Will you confess Him as Lord?" but, "*When* will you confess Him as Lord?" To confess Jesus Christ as Lord is to confess or agree that He is God!

b. As to its *motive* towards the Father—"to the glory of God the Father." The ultimate motive of all is God the Father's glory. He is glorified when Jesus is exalted! You honor the Father when you honor the Son! Romans 11:36 says, "For from Him and through Him and to Him are all things. To Him be the glory forever. Amen." He is the source, channel, and goal of all things! He alone is worthy of glory!

The principle of joy is that the pattern of your life must be conformed to Christ. This involves your acknowledgment of Christ's Person which we have now studied from Philippians 2:1-11. Our relationships with other believers will be deeply affected by following the marvelous example of Christ. He "emptied Himself" and "humbled Himself." And, of course, God has "highly exalted" Him! James 4:10 says, "Humble yourselves in the presence of the Lord, and He will exalt you."

STUDY QUESTIONS:

1. What would you say was the main problem among the Philippian believers according to these verses?

2. What should be our attitude toward others if we are truly reflecting the example of Christ?

3. What is the meaning of "He emptied Himself"?

4. In what ways is the deity of Christ taught in these verses?

5. Why has God the Father "highly exalted" the name of Jesus Christ?

6 PHILIPPIANS 2:12-18

+++

Your Application
of God's Purposes

+++

THE CHAPTER OUTLINED:

I. As to Our Responsibility
   A. Seen in the context
   B. Seen in their previous conduct
   C. Seen in Paul's command to them

II. As to God's Response
   A. The basic principle
   B. The prerequisite to working
   C. The pleasure He derives from this

III. As to Our Reactions
   A. In the way we do things
   B. In the witness we have in this world
   C. In the work we do in this world
   D. In the worth of our ministry to others

SUGGESTED BACKGROUND DEVOTIONAL READING

Monday—God Works All Things (Eph. 1:1-11)

Tuesday—Don't Complain (I Cor. 10:1-13)

Wednesday—Our Testimony (Matt. 5:10-16)

Thursday—Running the Race (I Cor. 9:19-27)

Friday—Laboring in Vain (I Cor. 15:51-58)

Saturday—Patience in the Race (Heb. 12:1-6)

Sunday—Our Joy (I Thess. 2:13-20)

The second factor related to the principle of joy we are studying in chapter 2 of Philippians is that we must apply in our lives the great purposes of God. If we expect the pattern of our life to be conformed to Christ, we must concentrate on what God wants to do in each of us. These verses comprise just one paragraph in the Greek language.

> So then, my beloved, just as you have always obeyed, not as in my presence only, but now much more in my absence, work out your salvation with fear and trembling; for it is God who is at work in you, both to will and to work for His good pleasure. Do all things without grumbling or disputing; that you may prove yourselves to be blameless and innocent, children of God above reproach in the midst of a crooked and perverse generation, among whom you appear as lights in the world, holding fast the word of life, so that in the day of Christ I may have cause to glory because I did not run in vain nor toil in vain. But even if I am being poured out as a drink offering upon the sacrifice and service of your faith, I rejoice and share my joy with you all. And you too, I urge you, rejoice in the same way and share your joy with me.

I. AS TO OUR RESPONSIBILITY — 2:12

We cannot remain passive to what God is doing in our lives. He expects us to "work out" what He "works in" us. There are three basic ways in which we understand our responsibility in applying the purposes of God in our lives.

A. Seen in the CONTEXT — "So then."

This verse is telling us that our responsibility to "work out" our salvation is based upon what was said in the immediate context of verses 1-11 of chapter 2. This would be the result of unity and responding to the marvelous example of Jesus Christ. Our joy in the Lord is deeply affected when there is disunity and lack of humility among believers. On that basis, plus the fact of Christ's example, we are exhorted to "work out" in our lives what is already "in" us. We have the potential of living in harmony with others and of demonstrating a life of humility because of God's life and work in us.

B. Seen in their previous CONDUCT—2:12.

The second way in which we understand our responsibility to apply the great purposes of God in our lives is to reflect upon the previous conduct of these Philippians. When they came to know the Lord, they manifested a real love and unity with humility one toward another.

1. Paul's *relationship* to them—"my beloved." Paul had a deep love for

these believers, and thus, the things which he urged them to be doing were spoken out of love, and not out of anger or disappointment.

2. Their *response* to him—"just as you have always obeyed, not as in my presence only, but now much more in my absence."

a. The *pattern* they established. Paul uses the word "always" and combines it with the word "obeyed." What a delightful remark about any believer that they had "always obeyed!" The word "obeyed" comes from the word "to hear" and the preposition "under." "To hear under" indicates a submissive ear, responding to the one "over" you. It is the word used in Ephesians 6:1 of children obeying their parents. Like a child to his father, these believers responded to the ministry of the Apostle Paul.

b. The *presence* of Paul. Not only had these believers responded to the Word of God when Paul was there in their midst, but they kept on growing in the Lord even when he was absent. On the basis of this wonderful response, Paul is now exhorting them to a continued unity, humility, and love that would truly reflect the example of Christ.

C. Seen in Paul's COMMAND to them—"work out your salvation with fear and trembling."

1. The *meaning* of this command. The words "work out" mean "to achieve; effect by labour or toil." The word "work" is put with the preposition meaning "down" or "according to." We are to work according to or in reference to our salvation. The "salvation" involved is the "salvation of yourselves." There are several possible views as to what this salvation means.

a. It may refer to eternal salvation. This would indicate that the believer has the ability to "achieve" this by his own efforts. Even though the next verse indicates the work of God in the believer, yet this statement in verse 12 would seem to teach some kind of effort on the part of the believer that would achieve his salvation.

b. It may refer to the practical evidence of eternal salvation. This view would emphasize that God is working it in us, and the proof that His salvation is really in us would be the way we are working it out in our daily lives. However, the words "work out" still carry the idea of achievement or effecting something by your labor or toil. While it may be the practical result of God's salvation that we are referring to, it would seem that our labor in that area would "achieve" the salvation we say God is working in us.

c. It may refer to the relationship of these believers one with another.

This view would take a restricted look at salvation from the standpoint of the context. The context of chapter 2 is dealing with the need of unity among the believers with special emphasis on humility and the example of Christ. The "salvation" that they are exhorted to "achieve" themselves would refer to their unity. This would emphasize again that there is an underlying problem in the church at Philippi of disunity and lack of humility, and as a result a loss of joy in the Lord. Paul is trying to deal with this before it becomes too serious. It seems that this latter view is better than the other views from the standpoint of the context. Verse 14 seems to emphasize this all the more.

2. The *manner* in which it should be done—"with fear and trembling." If the "salvation" refers to eternal salvation, it would then seem that the "fear and trembling" would indicate we better do this or else! As though we were in danger of losing it! When comparing the usage of these words "fear and trembling" we notice three particular examples.

a. I Corinthians 2:3—"And I was with you in weakness and in *fear and in much trembling.*" Paul's emphasis here was that his preaching was not characterized by great eloquence or persuasive words, but with an attitude of humility and inadequacy.

b. II Corinthians 7:15—"And his affection abounds all the more toward you, as he remembers the obedience of you all, how you received him with *fear and trembling.*" Paul is here referring to the ministry of Titus. He is not saying that they (Corinthian believers) were afraid of him, but was referring to an attitude of humility and a responsive heart to the ministry of Titus.

c. Ephesians 6:5—"Slaves, be obedient to those who are your masters according to the flesh, with *fear and trembling,* in the sincerity of your heart, as to Christ." In this passage, one could take the view that because it is a slave-to-master relationship, the words "fear and trembling" would mean to be afraid of what the master might do to the slave. However, upon closer observation, we see that the words "fear and trembling" are dealing with the Christian attitude and the response toward Christ. This concept of "obedience" or "submission" began in Ephesians 5:21-22 and is a result of the filling of the Holy Spirit (5:18-21). Three areas are given to illustrate this attitude of submission: wives to husbands (vv. 22-24); children to parents (6:1); and slaves to masters (6:5). The interpretation, therefore, would be that an attitude of submissiveness and humility is being urged upon these slaves.

After looking at the usage of these words, "fear and trembling," it appears that it is an attitude of humility and accountability to God that is being urged. The "salvation" would refer to the unity of the believers, and the attitude needed to accomplish this would be that of "fear and trembling."

II. AS TO GOD'S RESPONSE — 2:13

The second aspect of seeing how we should apply the purposes of God deals with God's response or what He is doing in our lives. The verse reads: "for it is God who is at work in you, both to will and to work for His good pleasure."

A. The basic PRINCIPLE. God is working in you!

That means there is hope for all of us in solving the problems we have. God is constantly working in us. The words "in you" could be interpreted two ways. One, it could mean the work of God in each individual believer, even though the word "you" is plural and not singular. Paul is writing to a group of believers. Or, it could refer to the unity among the believers as a group. A better translation might be that God is "working continuously among you." It is *God* who is working among you! This verse would be an encouragement to the believers in "achieving" this unity among themselves, knowing that God is working continually among them. His power is there and available!

B. The PREREQUISITE to working — "both to will and to work."

We often speak of the "will to work." Many of us simply don't "will" to do it, and that's why nothing is ever solved! God is the one working and also the one willing. The word "will" comes before the word "work," and that's the proper order. God puts the desire in our hearts. We are not naturally bent toward His purposes. We will "achieve" this unity among the believers because God works among us in giving us the desire and the ability to accomplish it! The emphasis upon *"both"* the willing and the working is a reminder of how we need to trust God in both areas of our desire as well as our deeds.

C. The PLEASURE He derives from this — "for His good pleasure."

In the Greek the preposition "for" literally means "in the behalf of." The reason why God is willing and working among us is in His own behalf. It is for His own pleasure. This one word "pleasure" is fundamental in describing why God made us in the first place! Revelation 4:11 tells us:

"Thou didst create all things, and because of Thy will they existed, and were created." God created because He wanted to do it! Ephesians 1:5 tells us that God "predestined us to adoption as sons through Jesus Christ to Himself, according to the kind intention [pleasure] of His will." The word "pleasure" comes from the word "well or good" and the word "to think." It means "to think well or good." It is not merely an understanding of what is good that is being stressed, but the willingness and freedom of one who desires to perform what is good. God is working among the believers for His own benefit and pleasure. He loves to do it. It brings glory to His name. "All things" are being worked for His glory and purpose! (Rom. 11:36).

III. AS TO OUR REACTIONS — 2:14-18

The third aspect of seeing how we should apply the purposes of God is by studying our reactions to this need for unity, humility, and love among the believers. We shall look at our reactions in four ways.

A. In the WAY we do things — 2:14 — "Do all things without grumbling or disputing."

This statement almost takes one by surprise after the words of verse 13! However, as we study the context we become more aware of the main thought of humility and unity among the believers of which these words form a very vital part. Nothing can destroy the unity of the believers any more than these two attitudes which result in very bad activities.

1. The *activities* we include—"do all things." The verb used here is a command and is in the present tense, indicating a continual habit of life. The meaning would be, "Constantly be doing all things." It doesn't matter what activity we are engaged in, we should do everything without "grumbling or disputing."

2. The *attitudes* we express—"without grumbling or disputing." The word translated "grumbling" (*goggusmon*) even sounds like grumbling when you pronounce the Greek word! It means to say something in a low tone. We would say it was like complaining "under your breath." I Corinthians 10:10 tells us that the Children of Israel did this in the wilderness. In Acts 6:1, this was the problem between the Hebrews and the Hellenistic Jews over the distribution to widows. I Peter 4:9 has an interesting usage of this in relationship to hospitality. Jude 16 uses the word in reference to false teachers who were always finding fault with others. When we are constantly complaining about things and finding fault with others it is

impossible for us to have the joy of the Lord. The word "disputing" (*dialogismon*) refers to inward reasoning or questioning. We get our word "dialogue" from this word. The word "logic" plus the preposition "through" carries the idea of thinking through things and coming out with a different opinion. It is used in a bad sense here to refer to the person who is always questioning and disagreeing with others. This person never has the joy of the Lord because he is looking for the opportunity to disagree or have another opinion. There is a time, of course, for other opinions to be shared, and disagreements to be discussed. But this verse is referring to one whose constant attitude is like this—they are always questioning things and others. If we want to have joy in all the activities we are called upon to do, we will heed this command to do "all things without grumbling or disputing."

B. In the WITNESS we have in this world – 2:15-16.

There is a very important reason why we should be doing all things without grumbling or disputing. Our testimony before the nonbeliever is at stake! When they see these attitudes reflected in the believer, they see no reason for becoming a Christian. Perhaps the most frequent opportunity we have in seeing this matter is at a place of employment where the believer must work alongside of nonbelievers. The attitudes that the believer has in his work are bearing tremendous impact upon the nonbelievers as they watch his testimony and try to determine what believing in Jesus Christ has done for him! But in the context of Philippians 2 it appears that the trouble is between believers. When nonbelievers see that believers cannot get along with one another, it cancels their Christian testimony! Jesus said in John 13:34-35, "A new commandment I give to you, that you love one another, even as I have loved you, that you also love one another. By this all men will know that you are My disciples, if you have love for one another." The real attraction to the "all men" is the love "for one another" among the believers! The first word of verse 15, "that" or "in order that" is a word of purpose. It tells us the reason behind the command of verse 14. We want to examine the issue of our witness to this world in three basic ways.

1. Seen in the *pattern* of life we should display. Two things reveal this pattern of life that should characterize the believer in his witness: "blameless and innocent." The word translated "prove" is the word to "become." We are being challenged to become blameless and innocent. Is that possible? After all, no one is perfect! Let's take a closer look at these two

words.

a. *Blameless.* The root word "to blame" is combined with the negative to mean "no blame" or "without blame." In the same verse we have a word that is sometimes confused with this one. In the words "above reproach" we have a word like the word meaning "blameless," but there is an important difference. The word translated "above reproach" is literally "without blemish." Christ our Lord was a lamb "without blemish"—that is, there was no sin in Him. However, He was blamed. Men brought charges against Him even though He had never sinned. It is possible to be blamed and yet be without blemish; it is also possible to have a blemish, and yet be unblamed. Many of us have sin in our lives that to this point has not been detected nor has any blame been brought against us, even though it is still sin and God knows it! Christ had no sin, and yet He was blamed. The point of this word in the context is that we are to be "without blame" in the matter of "grumbling or disputing" with one another so that our testimony before the nonbelievers is strong and attractive.

b. *Innocent.* The root word is "to mix," and with the negative it means "unmixed." It refers to the absence of any foreign substance. It was used in speaking of wine that was unmixed with water, and also of metals. Christ used the word in Matthew 10:16 in sending forth His disciples when He said, "Behold, I send you out as sheep in the midst of wolves; therefore be shrewd as serpents, and *innocent* as doves." Paul used it in Romans 16:19, "For the report of your obedience has reached to all; therefore I am rejoicing over you, but I want you to be wise in what is good, and *innocent* in what is evil." When our testimony for Christ is "mixed" with sinful practices or wrong motives it falls on deaf ears! The pattern of our life in this world should be characterized as "blameless and innocent."

2. Seen in the *problem* we face—"children of God above reproach in the midst of a crooked and perverse generation."

a. Our *relationship* to God—"children" (*tekna*). We are "born ones" into the family of God, and we bear His nature and life. We are representing our heavenly Father. Jesus told us in Matthew 5:16, "Let your light shine before men in such a way that they may see your good works, and glorify your Father who is heaven." It is difficult to live for Jesus in this wicked world. However, because of our relationship to Him, and because we are "born" of Him, we have His life in us, and thus, we have the potential of living a testimony before others that reflects His life.

b. Our *responsibility*—"above reproach." As we wrote above, this word means "without blemish." The issue of the context deals with our attitudes of "grumbling or disputing." In these matters there is to be no spot, stain, or blemish as we live in this crooked and perverse generation. The nonbeliever will "jump" at the opportunity to criticize our Christian experience when he sees the lack of unity and love among the believers.

c. The *resistance* we will experience—"in the midst of a crooked and perverse generation." The word "crooked" (*skolias*) is the opposite of the word "straight" (*orthos*). As a metaphor, it refers to being morally crooked, not straight on what the Bible teaches about sin and righteousness. The word "perverse" comes from the root word meaning "to twist or turn." Jesus referred to this kind of a generation in Matthew 17:17 and Luke 9:41. Paul spoke of certain false teachers who would come into the midst of the church and would speak "perverse things, to draw away the disciples after them" (Acts 20:30). This generation is morally crooked and never sees things as being "straight," and is constantly twisting things and turning aside from the truth of the Word. As believers, we have a constant battle in trying to bear a good testimony in that kind of environment. How foolish then for believers to be "grumbling and disputing" with one another! We have enough problems just facing this "generation" of unbelievers!

3. Seen in the *purpose* we should have—"among whom you appear as lights in the world, holding fast the word of life." The principle of joy in chapter 2 is that the pattern of our life must be conformed to Jesus Christ. This involves acknowledging His Person and life, and it involves our application of God's purposes. Some of us do not experience joy on a day-to-day basis because we forget the purpose God has for us in this wicked world we live in. This purpose involves two things according to these verses.

a. As to the *manifestation* we give to the world—"among whom you appear as lights in the world." The world is in darkness—moral and spiritual darkness. Satan has blinded their minds lest the light of the Gospel should shine unto them (II Cor. 4:3-4). God's purpose for the believer is to bring His "light" into a dark world. The words "among whom" would refer back to the word "generation." It is among more than one or two unbelievers that we are to "shine" as "lights." The word "lights" could be translated "luminaries" or "reflecting lights." We are not actually "lights" in the physical sense, but in the spiritual sense. Christ said that He was the "light of the world" (John 8:12). He told us that we were "lights" (Matt.

5:14-16). The "light" we have is spoken of in II Corinthians 4:6, "For God, who said, 'Light shall shine out of darkness,' is the One who has shone in our hearts to give the light of the knowledge of the glory of God in the face of Christ." It is the "light" of knowledge that we have—the knowledge of God's glory in Jesus Christ! A beautiful illustration of our responsibility to be "lights" in this world is seen when comparing the sun and the moon. The sun gives off its own light, but the moon simply reflects the light of the sun. Malachi 4:2 speaks of the "sun of righteousness" that will rise with "healing in its wings." Christ is like the "sun" in that He has inherent light. We are like the moon—reflecting lights. We reflect the light of Jesus Christ. The important thing that the world of unbelievers needs to see is the light of Jesus in us! The first phrase of verse 16 seems to describe what it means to be "lights" in this world.

b. As to the *message* we should proclaim—verse 16—"holding fast the word of life." The word "holding fast" means to "hold upon." It means to hold tightly or get a firm grip on it. The thing we are to hold on to is the word of life. The wonderful message that brings life! The words "holding fast" are in the present tense meaning to continue to hold fast. It should be a constant pattern of our life. If we are shining as "lights" in this spiritually dark world, then we are sharing the message of God's Word. There is a sense in which you can tell a Christian from a non-Christian by just looking at him. So often we see the scars of sin and unbelief on a person's countenance. But you cannot always tell! People will fool you! The real test is the message they speak. The "light" is the light of God's Word. In addition to the truth of God's Word, this passage is emphasizing the pattern of our life. What we do or don't do is reflecting upon the message we say we believe.

So far we have studied the importance of our reactions to God's purposes as to the way we do things and the witness we should bear in this world. Paul takes those thoughts and applies them to his own life in verses 16-18. He is looking at his own labor in their midst in terms of his pattern of life and the message he shared with them, and he is asking the question, "Is it really worth it all?"

C. In the WORK we do in this world — verse 16.

". . . so that in the day of Christ I may have cause to glory because I did not run in vain nor toil in vain."

1. The *reason* behind it—"so that in the day of Christ I may have cause to glory." This is a difficult phrase to translate literally from the Greek. It

says "unto boasting to me unto day of Christ." The preposition that begins this phrase carries the idea of result, and that is why the NASV translates it "so that." The word "boasting" refers to the ground or basis of boasting, and thus is translated "cause to glory." The "day of Christ" would refer to His second coming. Paul's meaning therefore, is that when Christ comes again, he was trusting that his pattern of life and message among them would give him reason for boasting when he saw the results in people saved through his ministry. It makes all the work of ministering the Word in this dark world worthwhile! Don't ever think that it is a waste of time to share the message of life with an unbelieving generation! God is using His Word. Some plant, and some water, but God is giving the increase! One day when Christ comes again we will see the fruit of our labors. Imagine the joy of seeing people in heaven whom you have shared the Word of God with down here on earth!

2. The *realization* of what is involved—"because I did not run in vain nor toil in vain."

a. With reference to our *efforts*—"run" and "toil." Make no mistake about this! There is work involved! The point is also on the fact that there is work to be done. To "run" is not to "walk." It suggests much more energy. The word translated "toil" comes from a root word meaning "to cut or strike" and refers to a striking or beating. It is used frequently in the New Testament to refer to laboring to the point of weariness or exhaustion.

b. With reference to our *expectations*—"not . . . in vain." The word "vain" (*kenon*) means "empty." Our efforts are not empty. They are going to be rewarded. I Corinthians 15:58 says, "Therefore, my beloved brethren, be steadfast, immovable, always abounding in the work of the Lord, knowing that your toil is not in vain in the Lord."

D. In the WORTH of our ministry to others – 2:17-18.

The first word of verse 17 is "but" and is a word of great contrast. Paul now proceeds to say that even if there is no future reward for him at the day of Christ, he still felt it was worth it to minister to their lives. The word "if" means "if and it is certain that this will be and is the case." You could translate it as "since."

1. The *nature* of that ministry to others—"I am being poured out as a drink offering upon the sacrifice and service of your faith." The word "to pour out as a drink offering" (*spendo*) could be simply pronounced into English from the Greek letters and you would get the idea of "spend."

Literally, we are often "spent" in our efforts. Paul used this same word in II Timothy 4:6 in facing his death—"For I am already being poured out as a drink offering, and the time of my departure has come." The area of ministry in which he felt this is described as being the "sacrifice" and "service" of your "faith." The word "sacrifice" refers to the things which are offered. In the Old Testament sacrificial system it would refer to the animal itself. Paul said in Romans 12:1, "I urge you therefore, brethren, by the mercies of God, to present your bodies a living and holy *sacrifice*, acceptable to God, which is your spiritual service of worship." The word "service" refers to the public office or duty that one has. Paul saw this matter of ministering to others as a duty he had and as a sacrifice that he was to make, and nothing was too great for His Lord and Saviour Jesus Christ! Even if there were no heavenly reward, it was still worth it in Paul's eyes! Is it in ours?

2. The *need* for rejoicing—"I rejoice and share my joy with you all. And you too, I urge you, rejoice in the same way and share your joy with me."

a. In the case of *Paul*—his testimony was that he was rejoicing. He had the joy of the Lord in ministering to others no matter what rewards were involved!

b. In the case of the *Philippians*—Paul urges them to do the same thing. We are not only to rejoice ourselves, but to share that joy with others. It's contagious! The basic point here is to rejoice in the privilege of ministering to others and in being ministered unto, regardless of the future reward!

If we really want the joy of the Lord we will learn to apply God's purposes for us in this world. God has a real purpose for you, Christian! He left you here on earth for a reason! He wants you to be a "light" in this dark world, and to share the message of His Word!

STUDY QUESTIONS:

1. What is the meaning of "salvation" when it says "work out your salvation" in Philippians 2:12?

2. According to verse 13, why is God working in us?

3. What is to be the pattern of our life in this world?

4. What is the main purpose of God for our lives in this world?

7 PHILIPPIANS 2:19-30

++

Your Appreciation
of God's People

++

THE CHAPTER OUTLINED:

   I. The Example of Timothy
      A. The purpose of his coming
      B. The pattern of life he demonstrated
      C. The proof of his faithfulness
      D. The prospect of his coming

  II. The Example of Epaphroditus
      A. The necessity of sending him to the Philippians
      B. The need of receiving him properly

SUGGESTED BACKGROUND DEVOTIONAL READING

Monday—Learning About Timothy (II Tim. 1:1-7)
Tuesday—Enduring Hardship (II Tim. 2:1-6)
Wednesday—If We Suffer (II Tim. 2:7-13)
Thursday—Advice to Timothy (II Tim. 2:19-26)
Friday—A Servant's Responsibility (II Tim. 4:1-8)
Saturday—Suffering with Others (I Cor. 12:18-26)
Sunday—Risking Our Lives (II Cor. 11:23-33)

This passage of Scripture is divided into two paragraphs—one dealing with Timothy, and the other with Epaphroditus. We learn much in this section about the importance of showing appreciation for God's people. We could have so much more joy in our Christian experience if we would learn to thank and praise God for people and express appreciation to them. There is too much in the way of critical remarks among believers. We are often tearing down instead of building up. Both of these men, Timothy and Epaphroditus, were outstanding servants of the Lord, and Paul loved them very much. His words in these verses are great lessons in how to encourage other believers in the Lord.

I. THE EXAMPLE OF TIMOTHY — 2:19-24

> But I hope in the Lord Jesus to send Timothy to you shortly, so that I also may be encouraged when I learn of your condition. For I have no one else of kindred spirit who will genuinely be concerned for your welfare. For they all seek after their own interests, not those of Christ Jesus. But you know of his proven worth that he served with me in the furtherance of the gospel like a child serving his father. Therefore I hope to send him immediately, as soon as I see how things go with me; and I trust in the Lord that I myself also shall be coming shortly.

A. The PURPOSE of his coming — 2:19.

1. Based on Paul's *expectation*—"But I hope in the Lord Jesus to send Timothy to you shortly." This expectation of Paul involves two important things for our learning:

a. His *submission* to the Lord's will. Paul's "hoping" was "in the Lord Jesus." Here's a beautiful way of expressing his trust and confidence in the Lord! This phrase, "in the Lord Jesus," could be looked upon as a basic motivation as well as an attitude of submission. Paul wanted what Jesus wanted!

b. His *sending* of Timothy. Some people see Paul exercising his apostolic office in this "sending" of Timothy. However the word "send" is not the root word from which we get our word "apostle." The word used here in verse 19 is a more general term than the word "apostle." The word "apostle" or "sent one" emphasizes a more specific mission or the role of an official who would represent a superior. This is not an authoritative sending, but rather a particular objective that would benefit Paul personally. Paul was sending a dear brother in the Lord who would be able to get information for him on how these believers at Philippi were getting along.

2. Based on the *encouragement* Paul wanted to receive—"so that I also

may be encouraged when I learn of your condition." The words "so that" are words of purpose. The specific reason why Paul wanted Timothy to visit them was so that Paul could then learn of their condition and thus receive encouragement. This suggests that Paul was a man of prayer and real concern. He did not forget these believers in Philippi, even though they were hundreds of miles away from him. The word "encouraged" (*eupsucheo*) comes from the word "well or good" and the word "soul." His soul would be well when he learned how they were getting along. No doubt he was very concerned about his children in the faith. His whole letter reveals that. He loved them dearly. The word "condition" is simply "the things concerning you." His interest in them was a real example of what he said back in verse 4: "Do not merely look out for your own personal interests, but also for the interests of others."

B. The PATTERN of life he demonstrated — 2:20-21.

Here Paul shares some wonderful insights as to the kind of person Timothy was, as well as the kind of person he himself was. Paul shows us the importance of showing and sharing appreciation of others, and Timothy reveals a real example of what Paul was describing in this book—one who was concerned about others and thus had the joy of the Lord.

1. In his *companionship* to Paul—"For I have no one else of kindred spirit." The words "kindred spirit" come from the word "equal" and the word "soul." As far as Paul knew, there was no one who felt the same way as he did for these believers in Philippi except Timothy. Their "souls" were "equal" in this respect. What a beautiful description of friendship! It reminds us of David and Jonathan in the Old Testament whose souls were knit together in love for each other. Paul was much older and more experienced and also was the spiritual father of Timothy. However, the spiritual child was now reflecting the concern of the spiritual father—"like father, like son."

2. In his *concern* for others—"who will genuinely be concerned for your welfare." The word "genuinely" is an adverb meaning "true or sincere." There was nothing false about Timothy. You could count on him to be real! Society today constantly teaches us to be phony and hypocritical; to put up a good front! The word "welfare" simply means "the things concerning you." Timothy had a sincere interest in the things concerning these believers. The word "concerned" is a very interesting word. It is usually used in a bad sense. The root word (*meridzo*) means "to divide." The word used here (*merimnesei*) usually emphasizes "anxious care" or

being "distracted." It is used in Luke 10:41 when Jesus said to Martha: "Martha, Martha, you are *worried* and bothered about so many things." But in our context here in Philippians 2 this word is used in a good sense in speaking of the concern of Timothy. The idea is to be distracted off of yourself and on to the needs of others. A proper concern for others means that you are more interested in their interests and needs than you are in yourself.

3. In *contrast* to others—3:21—"For they all seek after their own interests, not those of Christ Jesus." Timothy was the very opposite of most people who are usually self-centered and see little else. It shows us how Christ was now dominating the life and thinking of this man. There are two ways in which we see the contrast of Timothy's life to others.

a. As to *selfishness*—"For they all seek after their own interests." The word "interests" simply translates the words "the things of themselves." It is hard to imagine a more self-orientated remark—"they are continually seeking after the things of themselves." No wonder people have so little joy! Joy comes in giving of yourself to others. The more selfish we are, the less we experience real joy. Why is it so hard to learn that lesson? The answer is simple: because we are so selfish and self-centered! We just don't see it!

b. As to *service* to Christ—"not those of Christ Jesus." Timothy was different from others not only in the matter of selfishness, but also in the matter of his service. It was the interests of Jesus Christ that captivated his attention. To be interested in others, therefore, is to manifest a true service to Christ. Christ came not to be served, but to serve others. Timothy was manifesting the same characteristic in his life.

C. The PROOF of his faithfulness — 3:22.

Paul reminds these believers that they had known about Timothy from Paul's first visit to Philippi. Just before Paul went to Philippi he had picked up Timothy (Acts 16:1-3).

1. As to the *recognition* of it—"you know of his proven worth." The words "you know" mean that they continued to know about Timothy. They were constantly observing his pattern of life. The words "proven worth" refer to the process of proving something. Timothy's pattern of life was the process of proving the kind of person he really was. The Philippian believers knew much about Timothy already, and he had "proven" himself. They fully recognized his faithfulness in the ministry of the Gospel.

2. As to his *relationship* with Paul—"that he served with me in the furtherance of the gospel like a child serving his father." He served *with* Paul. The word "with" indicates a close companionship, a working together. The word "served" is the word meaning "to serve as a slave." A slave is one who is obedient to his master. Timothy had a submissive heart and life. In addition to that he mentioned that Timothy served him like a child to his father. The emphasis here is not only on submission, but also indicates a loving relationship. Timothy responded to Paul as a child to a father. Timothy was Paul's "son" in the faith. Paul wrote to him in I Timothy 1:2: "to Timothy, my true child in the faith," and in II Timothy 1:2: "to Timothy, my beloved son." The word "Timothy" means "to honor God," and we can certainly see why he did when we notice his submissive heart.

3. As to the *realm* in which he served—"in the furtherance of the gospel." The preposition could indicate motion or progress into the Gospel, or it might be translated "with reference to the gospel." Timothy had firsthand experience and he was able to learn from a great teacher. Paul said to him in II Timothy 2:2, "And the things which you have heard from me in the presence of many witnesses, these entrust to faithful men, who will be able to teach others also."

D. The PROSPECT of his coming— 2:23-24.

> Therefore I hope to send him immediately, as soon as I see how things go with me; and I trust in the Lord that I myself also shall be coming shortly.

Because of what Paul said about Timothy in verses 19-22, he had full confidence that Timothy would be just the one to visit these Philippians and to learn of their spiritual life and growth. The little word "therefore" shows us that it was because of the character of Timothy's life that Paul was ready to use him in this way. We can learn from this also that God is going to use the life that demonstrates these same qualities of submission and a responsive heart.

1. As to the *decision* regarding Paul—"as soon as I see how things go with me." In the construction of verses 23 and 24 there is the usage of two words that show a connection of thought between these verses (*men . . . de*). To read this into the translation, you would begin verse 23, "On the one hand," and begin verse 24, "but on the other hand." In verse 23 Paul says he is waiting on a decision regarding his current imprisonment; but in verse 24 he indicates that his trust is in the Lord. Paul is

confident that he would be released and come to them himself. Here is a beautiful combination of faith and a carefulness about presumption. The decision he was waiting for is described in the words "I see how things go with me." At the moment he sees what will happen, then he will send Timothy with the news. The verb means literally "to look away from" some things in order to see something else. As soon as Paul could look away from this, he would send Timothy. The word "immediately" indicates how soon he would send him upon hearing of the Roman decision. The word means literally "out of the same," referring to the same hour, or at once.

2. As to the *desire* of Paul—"I trust in the Lord that I myself also shall be coming shortly." This verse begins, "but on the other hand," meaning that Paul was not lacking in faith in this matter. He expected to be released, and come to see them.

II. THE EXAMPLE OF EPAPHRODITUS — 2:25-30

> But I thought it necessary to send to you Epaphroditus, my brother and fellow-worker and fellow-soldier, who is also your messenger and minister to my need; because he was longing for you all and was distressed because you had heard that he was sick. For indeed he was sick to the point of death, but God had mercy on him, and not on him only but also on me, lest I should have sorrow upon sorrow. Therefore I have sent him all the more eagerly in order that when you see him again you may rejoice and I may be less concerned about you. Therefore receive him in the Lord with all joy, and hold men like him in high regard; because he came close to death for the work of Christ, risking his life to complete what was deficient in your service to me.

The second example of showing appreciation to others which is a factor in our having the joy of the Lord is given to us in this portion of God's Word. The example is Paul's love and remarks for the man named Epaphroditus, who from the statement in verse 25 ("your messenger") appears to be a member of that church, and could quite possibly be its pastor. Perhaps he is one that Paul trained and discipled for that ministry in Philippi. We want to examine just two basic thoughts from these verses: One deals with the necessity of sending Epaphroditus to the Philippians; the other deals with the need of receiving him properly on the part of the Philippian believers.

A. The NECESSITY of sending him to the Philippians — 2:25-28.

Paul lists two basic reasons as to why he felt it such a necessity to send Epaphroditus to them.

1. To *relieve* their minds about his condition—2:25-27. Epaphroditus had become quite ill, and the Philippian believers were quite concerned. Paul is in jail, and Epaphroditus is seriously ill, and they thought they would never see either one of them again. They were losing their joy over these two circumstances. Paul was relieving their minds about these matters and in reference to Epaphroditus he accomplished this in three ways.

a. By *reminding* them of his qualities and service for God—2:25. "But I thought it necessary to send to you Epaphroditus, my brother and fellow-worker and fellow-soldier, who is also your messenger and minister to my need."

(1) This was based on a *decision* by Paul—"But I thought it necessary." The word "thought" means he thought it himself and made a specific decision. The reason for it is described by the word "necessary," which simply refers to what must needs be.

(2) This was also based on a *description* of his relationship to Paul—"my brother and fellow-worker and fellow-soldier."

(a) "Brother"—indicates the relationship to one another because they were both Christians, not earthly relatives.

(b) "Fellow-worker"—Epaphroditus was not one who sat on the sidelines while others did the work. He immediately joined with Paul in the work of the Gospel.

(c) "Fellow-soldier"—as Paul wrote to Timothy in II Timothy 2:3, "Suffer hardship with me, as a good soldier of Christ Jesus," so he commends Epaphroditus for his work as a "soldier." The Christian life is not a "bed of roses." There are battles to be fought, pressures to endure, conflicts to be overcome.

(3) This was also based on the *design* behind his coming to Paul in the first place—"who is also your messenger and minister to my need." The word "your" suggests that Philippi was his home.

(a) In relation to his *mission*—"your messenger." The word in Greek is the word "apostle" (*apostolon*). It indicates an official task. He was sent on this mission in an official way as an "apostle" or representative of the church in Philippi. It is possible that Epaphroditus could have been one of the apostles since there were others besides the twelve. However, it is probably more natural to take this as indicative of an official mission in behalf of the Philippian church.

(b) In relation to his *ministry*—"and minister to my need." This reveals that the Philippian church did care about Paul and what he was going through. Their hearts were saddened and they needed to discover the joy of the Lord in all of this, but it was this church that really cared for him. Paul will refer more to this matter in chapter 4. They responded when they learned of his "need."

b. By *revealing* his feelings toward the Philippians—2:26—"because he was longing for you all and was distressed because you had heard that he was sick." Paul here reveals some precious insights into the man Epaphroditus. This man was a living example of what Paul taught in Philippians 2:4, "do not merely look out for your own personal interests, but also for the interests of others." He was seriously ill, but he cared more about how these Philippian believers were taking this news. Paul revealed his feelings in two areas:

(1) As to his *desire*—"because he was longing for you all." The word "longing for" means to long for greatly. It's a strong word and refers to a deep, intense longing.

(2) As to his *distress*—"and was distressed." The word "distressed" seems to come from a root word meaning "knowing" and the negative "not." The idea is that he was concerned because he did not know how it was affecting them. He was more concerned about their reaction to his serious sickness than he was about himself. That's a tremendous point! As a pastor, I have seen people bear the same kind of testimony in the midst of very serious illness. I have seen a mother facing her own death by cancer be more concerned about how her children and loved ones were responding. Her joy in the Lord and concern for others did much to speak to my own heart. Epaphroditus is a good example for all of us! The first word in verse 26 is a conjunction that is translated in the NASV as "because." This word would suggest the specific cause behind Paul wanting to send Epaphroditus, and that was the deep concern and love for the Philippians that he saw in Epaphroditus. The words "was sick" which are repeated in verse 27 with a little more information, refer to a serious condition of weakness. The word means to be "without strength" or very "feeble." It is the same word used in James 5:14 and in John 11:4 of Lazarus.

c. By *reporting* on his true condition—2:27: "For indeed he was sick to the point of death, but God had mercy on him, and not on him only but also on me, lest I should have sorrow upon sorrow." Paul was trying to relieve the Philippian believers about the condition of Epaphroditus, and he did so by telling them of how God worked in a special way at a point when all seemed hopeless.

(1) The *extent* of his illness—"For indeed he was sick to the point of death." The word "indeed" could be also translated "even." Paul is telling them how sick he really was—"even to the point of death." The words "to the point of" combine the word "beside" or "alongside of" and the word "near," and the point is that Epaphroditus was laying alongside of and near death. It is interesting that the word for "sick" is often used in that regard of someone who is seriously ill. This should affect our interpretation of important passages like James 5:14-20 on anointing the sick with oil and praying for their healing. Every sickness would not be under consideration.

(2) The *expression* of God's intervention—"but God had mercy on him." Those are wonderful words—"but God!" Nothing is too hard for Him to do! God intervenes in a wonderful way and Epaphroditus becomes the recipient of God's "mercy." The words "had mercy on him" are in the aorist tense meaning that it was at a moment of time that God displayed mercy. We take that to mean the moment of his healing from this serious illness. In a moment of time God can heal what has been a growing and ever-worsening condition! Praise the Lord! He "is able to do exceeding abundantly beyond all that we ask or think, according to the power that works within us" (Eph. 3:20).

(3) The *effect* upon Paul—"and not on him only but also on me, lest I should have sorrow upon sorrow." We learn here of the deep affection which Paul had for Epaphroditus. It would have been another "sorrow" for Paul to bear had God not intervened and healed Epaphroditus. The word for "sorrow" is the root word meaning "pain or grief in mind or body." The Lord knows how much "pain" we can suffer, and He will never give us more than we can bear. Paul saw this healing of his friend as "mercy" from God for his own life. It must have been a great encouragement to Paul to see God work so wonderfully in healing Epaphroditus.

The first reason why Paul felt it was a necessity to send Epaphroditus to the Philippian believers was to relieve their minds about his true condition. The second reason is stated here in verse 28.

2. To *rejoice* when they saw him—2:28—"Therefore I have sent him all the more eagerly in order that when you see him again you may rejoice and I may be less concerned about you." This group of believers was losing its joy. Paul knew that the presence of Epaphroditus in their midst would return that joy to them. Paul cared about the spiritual growth of these believers, and he saw that sending his dear friend would be of great help to

their maturity at this time. The words "all the more eagerly" means with "haste; speed; or diligence." Paul would waste no time in sending him. The words "when you see" mean that upon the moment of seeing him, they might rejoice! Just seeing him again would bring joy to their hearts! Paul's words "and I may be less concerned about you" show us that he had a personal motive in sending Epaphroditus. He fully trusted this man and knew that he would accomplish in their lives what was needed at this time. He would be greatly relieved. The root word translated "less concerned" is from the same word translated "sorrow" in verse 27. It means "no pain or grief." Their joy would mean the removal of a burden from his heart.

B. The NEED of receiving him properly — 2:29-30.

> Therefore receive him in the Lord with all joy, and hold men like him
> in high regard; because he came close to death for the work of Christ,
> risking his life to complete what was deficient in your service to me.

The word "therefore" would connect this final admonition with the preceding verses which demonstrate the kind of man that Epaphroditus was. In the light of this, they were to properly receive him when he came.

1. As to their *relationship* to the Lord—"receive him in the Lord." They were brothers and sisters in Christ. They were to receive him as a believer, but more than that, they were to receive him in the "spirit" of the Lord Himself. How would the Lord welcome him home?

2. As to their *rejoicing*—"with all joy." There wasn't to be any hesitancy on their part when he came. Paul admonishes them to welcome him with open arms! He knew how much Epaphroditus loved them.

3. As to their *regard* for him—"and hold men like him in high regard." A man like Epaphroditus comes along once in a lifetime! They are being admonished to show their appreciation for such a man. They were to constantly hold him in honor. Certainly these verses are not telling us to give undue honor to men, nor to honor them above our Lord Jesus Christ. However, they do speak of showing honor to whom it is due as Romans 13:7 verifies. Too often we do not show appreciation toward fellow believers that we ought to, and as a result, we do not have the joy we could have. We often criticize and tear down instead of encourage and build up.

4. As to the *reason* behind this instruction—2:30—"Because he came close to death for the work of Christ, risking his life to complete what was deficient in your service to me." The reason behind this admonition to receive him with joy and with honor is based on two things.

a. It is based on the *danger* he experienced for the cause of Christ. One might say "that because of" or "that on account of." It is strongly emphasizing that this is the reason he deserves a warm welcome and a grand reception when he comes.

(1) The *motivation* he had—"the work of Christ." What made Epaphroditus the kind of man he was? He was motivated by the work of Christ. One could say that it was because of what Christ did for him, but more likely it refers to working for Christ, doing His will and work in this world. This phrase teaches us that this man was submitted to God's Word and will.

(2) The *manner* in which this danger was described—"risking his life to complete what was deficient in your service to me" and "close to death." The words "close to death" mean "until death he was near." His serious illness appears to be the result of the "work of Christ." He labored long and hard for Christ and his body was now unable to keep going. When a man goes this far in his service for Christ, the least we could do is receive him with joy and in honor! How little appreciation we often show to God's faithful workers all over the world! Consider how tragic is the average missionary's return home! If he is "fortunate" he will get an opportunity to speak in his church, and people will often wear him out in their efforts to appear concerned about his work. But what about him? It ought to be a grand experience for God's faithful workers to return home! There should be much joy and much honoring of their faithful service! There should be great concern for him as a person and every effort should be made to properly receive him and welcome him home!

The words "risking his life" mean to "throw aside" or "to expose oneself to danger" or "to hazard." The word "life" is the Greek word for "soul" (*psuche*). It reminds us of the words of I John 3:16, "We know love by this, that He laid down His life for us; and we ought to lay down our lives for the brethren." The word "lives" is the word "souls." Is this verse advocating martyrdom? Or, is it rather speaking of laying aside selfish interest and pursuit for the benefit of the one we are trying to share love with? Epaphroditus "hazarded" his life for the cause of Christ and the people to whom he ministered.

b. It was based on the *deficiency* of their service—"to complete what was deficient in your service to me." The word "complete" means "to fill up." The Philippian believers had only started in their service and ministry to Paul, and Paul says that Epaphroditus risked his life to fill up the cup of service that they should have filled. The word "deficient" comes from a verb meaning "to be behind." They were behind in their efforts to serve Christ and minister to Paul. They were lacking in spiritual growth and certainly in the joy of the Lord.

The basic thought of these verses (Phil. 2:19-30) is that of appreciation for God's people. We not only learn important qualities in the lives of Timothy and Epaphroditus to emulate, but we also learn much from Paul about showing our appreciation for what God is doing in others. It can bring back the joy of the Lord if we will learn to encourage rather than discourage; to build up rather than tear down; to honor rather than to criticize. May God fill us with His joy!

STUDY QUESTIONS:

1. Why was Paul so confident of the ministry of Timothy?

2. How did Paul describe his relationship with Timothy?

3. What qualities does Epaphroditus reveal that we need in our lives?

4. How were the Philippian believers to receive Epaphroditus when he returned to them? Why?

Principles of Joy

++

PRINCIPLE NO. 3

THE PURPOSE OF YOUR LIFE MUST BE CONTROLLED BY JESUS CHRIST

Philippians 3:1-21

KEY VERSE: Philippians 3:10—"That I may know Him, and the power of His resurrection and the fellowship of His sufferings, being conformed to His death."

8 PHILIPPIANS 3:1-7

‡‡

Your Approach
Toward Your Past

‡‡

THE CHAPTER OUTLINED:

I. **The Basic Principle**
   A. The command involved
   B. The character of it

II. **The Problems We Face**
   A. As to the reason for writing about them
   B. As to the realization of them
   C. As to the recognition of the true teachers

III. **The Past To Forget**
   A. Seen in Paul's comparison to others
   B. Seen in the character of Paul's life
   C. Seen in the concern he had for these things

SUGGESTED BACKGROUND DEVOTIONAL READING

Monday—Paul before Christ (Acts 7:58—8:4)

Tuesday—Paul at Conversion (Acts 9:1-9)

Wednesday—God Chooses Paul (Acts 9:10-19)

Thursday—Paul, a New Christian (Acts 9:20-30)

Friday—Paul's Religious Background (Acts 22:1-16)

Saturday—Paul the Pharisee (Acts 23:1-11)

Sunday—Testimony to Agrippa (Acts 26:1-18)

The third principle of joy which we are studying in the Book of Philippians is that *The Purpose of Your Life Must Be Controlled by Christ.* Paul beautifully expresses this in Philippians 3:10 which is the key verse of this principle and of this chapter. "To know Him" is the center of Christianity. Christianity is Christ! Upon receiving Christ as our Lord and Saviour, we often plunge into a state of learning that concentrates upon what we can do to have assurance, joy, peace, love, and purpose in our lives. We put the emphasis on the "how-to's" of Christian life and growth. However, we often overlook or just neglect the main purpose of the believer which is to know Jesus Christ!

In the first seven verses Paul tells us that if our purpose in life is being controlled by Christ then this will involve our approach toward our past. Some of us spend too much time thinking about the past and even glorying in it! Today is the first day of the rest of your life! Paul had many reasons to glory in his past record, but he uses his own example to exhort us to forget the past and to move on to Christian growth and maturity in knowing Christ and in anticipating our being with Him in heaven forever!

> Finally, my brethren, rejoice in the Lord. To write the same things again is no trouble to me, and it is a safeguard for you. Beware of the dogs, beware of the evil workers, beware of the false circumcision; for we are the true circumcision, who worship in the Spirit of God and glory in Christ Jesus and put no confidence in the flesh, although I myself might have confidence even in the flesh. If anyone else has a mind to put confidence in the flesh, I far more: circumcised the eighth day, of the nation of Israel, of the tribe of Benjamin, a Hebrew of Hebrews, as to the Law, a Pharisee; as to zeal, a persecutor of the church; as to the righteousness which is in the Law, found blameless. But whatever things were gain for me, those things I have counted as loss for the sake of Christ.

I. THE BASIC PRINCIPLE — 3:1

Paul begins this section with the word "finally," and you would think that he is about ready to conclude the letter. The word simply means "the rest" or "the remaining." It is like a summary statement to all the things he is sharing with them.

A. The COMMAND involved—"rejoice in the Lord."

This command emphasizes that we should be constantly rejoicing. Continual joy ought to be the posesssion of every believer! We have every reason to be joyful!

B. The CHARACTER of it—"in the Lord."

Perhaps the reason why we are not experiencing constant joy is because we have not learned the sphere in which we are to rejoice. We are not told here to rejoice in circumstances, difficulties, problems, or blessings, but "in the Lord." Other passages (like Rom. 5:3-5 and James 1:2-4) tell us to look upon our trials and difficulties with joy knowing what they will produce in our lives in the way of maturity. But apart from Christ, there will be no abundant joy! Psalm 16:11 tells us: "Thou wilt make known to me the path of life; in Thy presence is fulness of joy; in Thy right hand there are pleasures forever." To rejoice in the Lord is the key to the message of the Book of Philippians! When we set our minds and affections upon Christ and seek to know Him, we will experience more joy in our lives. He is our joy! He will fill your heart with joy!

II. THE PROBLEMS WE FACE — 3:1-3

The basic problem that Paul is referring to deals with the influence and teaching of a group of people commonly referred to as "Judaizers." These people insisted on the obligations of the Mosaic law as being binding upon the believer. They were legalists, and they were constantly attacking the ministry of Paul and contradicting the message of God's grace and Christian liberty. They were proud of their Jewish heritage, but when exposed to the gospel of grace, they also felt that Gentile Christians should conform to the standards they knew in Judaism, such as circumcision, and so forth. After all, it was the sign of the Abrahamic covenant, the covenant which teaches the salvation of Gentiles through the Jewish line (Gen. 12:3—"and in you all the families of the earth shall be blessed"). However, as Paul argued in Romans 4:9-13:

> Is this blessing then upon the circumcised, or upon the uncircumcised also? For we say, 'Faith was reckoned to Abraham as righteousness.' How then was it reckoned? While he was circumcised, or uncircumcised? Not while circumcised, but while uncircumcized; and he received the sign of circumcision, a seal of the righteousness of the faith which he had while uncircumcised, that he might be the father of all who believe without being circumcised, that righteousness might be reckoned to them, and the father of circumcision to those who not only are of the circumcision, but who also follow in the steps of the faith of our father Abraham which he had while uncircumcised. For the promise to Abraham or to his descendants that he would be heir of the world was not through the Law, but through the righteousness of faith.

It is obvious that Abraham believed God before he was circumcised (about

11 years before). You might say that Abraham was saved by faith as a Gentile before he ever became a Jew or recognized as such by circumcision. However, the simplest thing we can see is that circumcision was not a requirement in the case of Abraham as to his being declared righteous by God. That was based on faith alone.

A. As to the REASON for writing about them — 3:1.

"To write the same things again is no trouble to me, and it is a safeguard for you."

1. With reference to *Paul*—"is no trouble to me." Paul was fully able to handle the opposition and teaching of these Judaizers. The word "trouble" comes from the root word "to shrink." Paul was not shrinking in this matter. In Matthew 25:26 this word is translated "lazy," and in Romans 12:11, "not lagging behind."

2. With reference to the *Philippians*—"it is a safeguard for you." The word "safeguard" is a combination of the negative "not" and the word "to trip up." The point is that this instruction would help these believers not to trip up or stumble over this false teaching.

B. As to the REALIZATION of them — 3:2.

"Beware of the dogs, beware of the evil workers, beware of the false circumcision." The word "beware" means "to see" or "watch" or "take heed." Paul is commanding them to be on constant alert. They are to be continually watching out for these false teachers. He describes them in three ways:

1. "Dogs"—the Jews used this term in referring to the Gentiles. Revelation 22:15 speaks: "Outside are the dogs and the sorcerers and the immoral persons and the murderers and the idolaters, and every one who loves and practices lying." Deuteronomy 23:18 says: "You shall not bring the hire of a harlot or the wages of a dog into the house of the Lord your God for any votive offering, for both of these are an abomination to the Lord your God." Obviously, the term "dogs" is a term of rebuke and disrespect. Those Jewish teachers who read this were to say the least— unhappy! The passage in Deuteronomy is a condemnation of offering "wages" to the Lord that were acquired in a wrong way, such as in male prostitution. Paul associates that Old Testament usage of "dog" with these false teachers and insinuates that God is not pleased with them either, no matter what they try to make others believe about their dedication to the Mosaic law.

2. "Evil workers"—There are two basic words for "evil." One means "evil in influence or effect," and the other used in our text here means "evil in character." The emphasis here is on the fact that they were evil workers in character and nature. Perhaps the point would deal with their motivations in what they were doing.

3. "False circumcision"—This is an obvious play-on-words by the Apostle Paul. The word translated "false circumcision" means literally "the cutting off." The King James Version translates this word "concision," meaning "the cutting." When you circumcise a child it involves the cutting of the foreskin of the penis. Paul refers to those who would insist on the necessity of Gentile believers being circumcised as "those who would cut off." He doesn't honor them with the word "circumcision," but rather uses a word to rebuke them. They were only interested in the outward conformity of an individual to a physical rite or practice. They failed to understand that the righteousness we have before God is based on faith alone.

C. As to the RECOGNITION of the true teachers — 3:3.

"For we are the true circumcision, who worship in the Spirit of God and glory in Christ Jesus and put no confidence in the flesh." The word "circumcision" means "to cut around," whereas the word "false circumcision" in verse 2 mean "to cut down or off." Romans 2:25-29 tells us of the true circumcision:

> For indeed circumcision is of value, if you practice the Law; but if you are a transgressor of the Law, your circumcision has become uncircumcision. If therefore the uncircumcised man keep the requirements of the Law, will not his uncircumcision be regarded as circumcision? And will not he who is physically uncircumcised, if he keeps the Law, will he not judge you who though having the letter of the Law and circumcision are a transgressor of the Law? For he is not a Jew who is one outwardly; neither is circumcision that which is outward in the flesh; but he is a Jew who is one inwardly; and circumcision is that which is of the heart, by the Spirit, not by the letter; and his praise is not from men, but from God.

How sad that people do not recognize the difference between the "inward" and the "outward"! One can perform all the religious rituals possible and yet still not be a true believer! True circumcision is of the heart and of the Spirit. Paul gives us three ways to tell the "true circumcision":

1. By their *manner* of worship—"who worship in the Spirit of God." The word "worship" means "to serve or to render religious service." Paul

used the word in Romans 1:9 when he said: "For God, whom I serve in my spirit." The contrast is to serve "in the flesh." Those who are the true circumcision do not worship God with outward ceremonies and practices, but in the "inner man," or "in the Spirit of God." The phrase could also be translated "by the Spirit of God." Either way it is good. We should worship by means of the Spirit of God and in the realm of the Spirit, in contrast to the flesh.

2. By their *motivation*—"and glory in Christ Jesus." The word "glory" is a present tense and emphasizes the fact that the true circumcision does not glory in outward ceremonies and rites, but constantly glories in Christ. He is the center of it all! Many people today who claim to be religious and who claim the name of "Christian" do nothing more than glory in their church membership, baptism, works, rituals, religious activities, and the like. You can recognize the true circumcision as those who glory in the Person and work of Jesus Christ.

3. By their *methods*—"and put no confidence in the flesh." The third way by which you can tell the true teachers is that they do not put trust and confidence in carnal methods and practices. People who emphasize that and ignore Christ are false teachers and lead believers astray. The outward physical rite of circumcision will never bring the proper assurance to the heart of your relationship to Jesus Christ, and neither will any other outward practice. It is the Spirit of God that brings that assurance or confidence. Romans 8:16 says, "The Spirit Himself bears witness with our spirit that we are children of God." The flesh cannot give confidence nor should we put confidence in it. Our trust is to be centered in the Person and work of Jesus Christ.

III. THE PAST TO FORGET — 3:4-7

In order to really experience joy today in living for Christ, one must continue to forget the achievements of the past. Many people in remembering former days fail to be motivated about serving Christ today. Christians often rely on what they did for Christ in the past and keep telling others about these achievements. And yet, they fail to serve Christ today and as a result, have little joy. It often becomes an excuse for our present apathy or indifference to Christ and His work. We remind ourselves of the past in order to soothe our conscience about present struggles, problems, or discouragements. Paul had many reasons to glory in his past from a human point of view, but he clearly shows us that the past is to be put behind us, and we are to look forward to what lies ahead.

A. Seen in Paul's COMPARISON to others — 3:4.

". . . although I myself might have confidence even in the flesh. If anyone else has a mind to put confidence in the flesh, I far more." Paul here interprets the meaning of having "confidence in the flesh" as pride in real facts about one's background. According to the verses that follow it is a pride in religious background as well as national and family background. Many Jews of Paul's day believed they were saved by the simple fact that they were born Jews, circumcised, and followed the Mosaic Law. But Paul clearly teaches in all his writings that the Gospel preached to Abraham and the one that Abraham believed was a Gospel based upon faith. Both in the Old Testament as well as the New Testament the Bible teaches salvation by faith in the Messiah for what He has done for us. Paul would not take a "back-seat" to anyone in terms of possible "confidence in the flesh." He had everything going for him. Surely Paul was "saved," wasn't he? Not until he met Jesus on the Damascus road (Acts 9) was he saved. All of Paul's tremendous background and religious knowledge could not have saved him! Paul says literally, "If any other [person] is thinking to have confidence in flesh, I more." Are you trusting in your family or religious background? It cannot save you! Only Jesus can do that!

B. Seen in the CHARACTER of Paul's life — 3:5-6.

Circumcised the eighth day, of the nation of Israel, of the tribe of Benjamin, a Hebrew of Hebrews, as to the Law, a Pharisee; as to zeal, a persecutor of the church, as to the righteousness which is in the Law, found blameless.

These verses read like a "Who's Who" among religious people! What a background this man had! Surely this would guarantee his standing before God, wouldn't it? Of course, Paul's answer to that is not only "no," but also that he counted all of these things but loss in comparison to the wonderful knowledge of Jesus Christ! There are seven statements here about Paul's life which cover the common views of people about what gains the favor of God.

1. As to *ritual*—"circumcised the eighth day." This was the exact day after the birth of a male child that the rite of circumcision should take place. It also emphasizes that Paul was not a son of Ishmael. The Ishmael-ites circumcised their children on the thirteenth day (Gen. 17:25). Isaac, the son of the promise (Heb. 11:17-18), was circumcised on the eighth day (Gen. 21:4), and this was commanded by God. Paul would also be point-

ing out that he was not a Gentile convert who would be circumcised after converting to Judaism. The main point of Paul's reference to this rite of circumcision is to prove to these false teachers who demanded that the Gentile believers be circumcised in order to guarantee their salvation that it did not save him. Paul teaches that circumcision will not save you. Abraham was saved before circumcision and Paul after, but both teach the same thing. This truth is that a man is counted righteous before God on the basis of faith, not circumcision.

2. As to *national relationship*—"of the nation of Israel." The word "nation" (*genous*) is the word "generation" from which we get "genealogy." Paul could trace his genealogy, and these Jewish records were kept and were still available up until the destruction of Jerusalem in A.D. 70. From a human standpoint, one can understand the importance of the statement of Paul that he was of the "nation of Israel."

It is interesting to talk today with Jewish young people (called "sabra" after a cactus-type plant with a fruit that is said to be "prickly on the outside, but sweet on the inside") who have been born in the land of Israel since 1948. You can feel the pride and nationalism in these young people. They have every right to be proud and it makes one desire to be one of them. However, no matter how thrilling from a human point of view this national background is, it will not save you. Only Jesus can do that! The first mention and establishment of the word "Israel" comes from Genesis 32:28 where Jacob's name was changed to "Israel," and his children came to be called "the sons of Israel," of which there developed 12 tribes. In the first statement, "circumcised the eighth day," he eliminated the fact that he was an Ishmaelite instead of a son of Isaac. In this next statement, "of the nation of Israel," he eliminates those who trace their descent through Esau, the other son of Isaac. In every way Paul was showing how above many others, he would have every reason to feel secure and confident about his religious background.

3. As to *tribal relationship*—"of the tribe of Benjamin." Out of the 12 tribes of Israel, Paul could trace his family line back through the tribe of Benjamin. From a Jewish point of view, this was worth mentioning. Benjamin was the youngest son of Jacob, and the son, along with Joseph, whom he loved dearly. He was born of Rachel as was Joseph. The first king of Israel, Saul, was from this tribe, and Paul's original name was the same. It was also the only tribe that stayed with the tribe of Judah, the tribe of David, when the kingdom was split between the 10 tribes of the north who

followed Jeroboam, and the two tribes of the south who followed Reho-
boam, the son of Solomon. From a Jewish point of view, this was very
commendable. The very term "Jews" is based on the word "Judah." This
identification with Benjamin eliminated Paul's being a part of the 10
northern tribes in terms of family background. His family was loyal to the
throne of David.

4. As to *cultural relationship*—"a Hebrew of Hebrews." Paul narrows
down his relationships even further as he declares that he is a real Hebrew.
The statement would emphasize that he was not a mixture in terms of his
parental line, and also that he was not a Hellenistic Jew (a Jew absorbed in
Greek culture and language). It no doubt refers also to his linguistic
ability. In Acts 21:37-40 we have an interesting insight into Paul's background and ability. Paul spoke Greek according to verse 37 when he spoke
with the Roman commander. However, when he spoke to the people of
Jerusalem, he used the Hebrew dialect. Some believe that this is a reference to the use of Aramaic (a cognate language to Hebrew) in Palestine
during the first century A.D. Acts 22:2 states, "And when they heard that
he was addressing them in the Hebrew dialect, they became even more
quiet." Paul then went on to tell them of his background and the interesting fact is brought out in Acts 22:3 that he was "brought up in this city,
educated under Gamaliel." Paul had many advantages going for him as far
as the Jews were concerned. He was no half-breed, and certainly not a
Samaritan with whom the Jews had no dealings. From a linguistic and
cultural point of view, he had much to commend him in the eyes of the
Jews. How strange it must have been for these Judaizers (Jewish teachers
who insisted on circumcision for Gentile believers) to hear a man like Paul
say that all of this background is worthless when compared with the
knowledge of Jesus Christ!

5. As to *religion*—"as to the Law, a Pharisee." When one reads the
rebukes of Jesus toward the "scribes and Pharisees" (Matt. 23:13-36), it is
hard to believe that a Pharisee was to be commended or respected. Christ
certainly exposed them for their mere external righteousness. However, we
must never forget that these Pharisees were sincere and extremely devoted
to the Mosaic Law. They would be comparable to the Orthodox Jews of
today. They studied the Old Testament carefully, and were very concerned
about obedience to God's law. In Luke 18:9-14 Jesus gave us some interesting information about these religious leaders. In speaking of the
Pharisee who went up to the temple to pray we read: "The Pharisee stood

and was praying thus to himself, 'God I thank Thee that I am not like other people, swindlers, unjust, adulterers, or even like this tax-gatherer. I fast twice a week; I pay tithes of all that I get.' " Certainly they were to be commended for these outward displays of religious devotion. The problem was just that—it was an outward display only! Jesus said in Matthew 23:2-3: "The scribes and Pharisees have seated themselves in the chair of Moses; therefore all that they tell you, do and observe, but do not do according to their deeds; for they say things, and do not do them."

Jesus Christ continually pointed out to us the real problem of the Pharisee. They did things, as good as they were, to be seen of others. They exalted themselves before others; they were proud of their religious devotion. One of their number, a man named Nicodemus, came to Jesus by night and although he was according to Jesus "the teacher of Israel" (John 3:10), yet he did not understand what Jesus was teaching. These men were concerned with teaching God's law and following it, but they missed the need of humility and a changed heart on the inside; they concentrated on external righteousness.

Paul mentioned in Acts 22:3 that he was "educated under Gamaliel, strictly according to the law of our fathers." Gamaliel was a Pharisee and well respected by everyone (Acts 5:34). In Acts 23:6 Paul said, "Brethren, I am a Pharisee, a son of Pharisees." The plural word "Pharisees" would refer to the line of Pharisees, going back to his grandfather at least. With all this background, you would think that above all people Paul would certainly be saved! After all, how could one have so much knowledge and religious background and not be saved? And that, friends, is the real tragedy in many people's thinking! We assume that a great religious knowledge, combined with outward adherence to the principles of God's law, must be proof that a man is accepted by God and definitely saved! Jesus said concerning these Pharisees in Matthew 5:20, "For I say to you, that unless your righteousness surpasses that of the scribes and Pharisees, you shall not enter the kingdom of heaven." That ought to settle it once for all! More is needed than great religious knowledge and outward moral behavior! The need is Jesus! Without His righteousness, there is no true righteousness!

6. As to *resistance* to the Christian movement—"as to zeal, a persecutor of the church." The word "persecutor" indicates he was constantly persecuting the church. Paul was very active in his resistance to Christianity and all in the name of God! He believed that he was doing the right thing. Of

all people, Paul ought to have confidence before God for his religious zeal, at least that's what most Jews would conclude! But even this was not enough! As a matter of fact, as Paul learned on the Damascus road, he was attacking Jesus by attacking the church. Acts 9:4: "and he fell to the ground, and heard a voice saying to him, 'Saul, Saul, why are you persecuting me?' " And in verse 5, Paul said, "Who art Thou, Lord?" and the voice answered, "I am Jesus whom you are persecuting." It was Paul (Saul of Tarsus) who stood by while Stephen was stoned. Some have suggested since the robes of those who stoned him were laid at Saul's feet, that Saul was the one administering this terrible deed. We know from Acts 8:1 that he was in "hearty agreement" with the stoning of Stephen which resulted in his death. Acts 8:3 says: "But Saul began ravaging the church, entering house after house and dragging off men and women, he would put them in prison." Such zeal this religious Pharisee had! Saul was not satisfied with his work in Jerusalem but according to Acts 9:1-2 was anxious to pursue his efforts to Damascus.

In Acts 22:19 when Paul reviews his story before the Jews he said, "And I said, 'Lord, they themselves understand that in one synagogue after another I used to imprison and beat those who believed in Thee.' " In Acts 26:10-11 Paul tells us, "And this is just was I did in Jerusalem; not only did I lock up many of the saints in prisons, having received authority from the chief priests, but also when they were being put to death I cast my vote against them. And as I punished them often in all the synagogues, I tried to force them to blaspheme; and being furiously enraged at them, I kept pursuing them even to foreign cities." There is no doubt from all of this evidence that Paul was extremely dedicated to the Jewish cause and of all people, he demonstrated all the qualities and characteristics of one who should have complete confidence before God. And yet, all of this was like garbage in comparison to what he found in Jesus Christ!

7. As to the *righteousness* in the law—"as to the righteousness which is in the Law, found blameless." Here is an amazing statement by Paul! In what sense was he "found blameless?" The word "blameless" refers to the fact that there was no legal charge against him. It doesn't mean that he never sinned. When he did sin, he brought the appropriate sacrifice. Paul did everything in the eyes of others that the law demanded. As far as others were concerned, Paul was "blameless."

It is clear from this statement by Paul that there are two kinds of righteousness. One is external; the other, internal. One is based on the works of a man; the other, upon his faith. One is a practical righteousness in terms of doing things that are right; the other, a positional righteousness that is based upon what Jesus Christ has done at the cross. Of course, when one accepts God's righteousness, there will be evidence of a practical righteousness in his life (I John 2:29). But that is the product of God's righteousness, not the result of human works and achievement. Paul spoke of this problem in Romans 10:1-4:

> Brethren, my heart's desire and my prayer to God for them is for their salvation. For I bear them witness that they have a zeal for God, but not in accordance with knowledge. For not knowing about God's righteousness, and seeking to establish their own, they did not subject themselves to the righteousness of God. For Christ is the end of the law for righteousness to everyone who believes.

All of these seven statements about Paul's illustrious past reveal one major truth. It is not by works that we are saved! It is not by family descent or religious heritage! It is by Christ alone! So many people today are still trying to establish their own righteousness. As Isaiah 64:6 says, "For all of us have become like one who is unclean, and all our righteous deeds are like a filthy garment; and all of us wither like a leaf, and our iniquities, like the wind, take us away." Romans 3:10 says: "There is none righteous, not even one." No man can be right before God apart from trusting in the finished work of Jesus Christ at the cross. That's why Paul could say that all of these things he counted as loss for Christ. They had no value with God anyway!

We will not have much joy in our lives if we continue to trust in these things instead of in Jesus Christ. Remember that our principle of joy in chapter 3 is that the purpose of our lives must be controlled by Christ, and that involves our approach toward our past and all its accomplishments.

C. Seen in the CONCERN he had for these things – 3:7.

"But whatever things were gain to me, those things I have counted as loss for the sake of Christ." Here is the culmination of this passage—"things" versus "Christ." Paul had made his choice. Have you?

1. As to personal *worth*—he described these "things" as possible "gain." It comes from the verb meaning "to make a profit." It is used in James 4:13 when it says, "Come now, you who say, 'Today or tomorrow, we shall go to such and such a city, and spend a year there and engage in business and *make a profit.*' " Paul has already used this word in reference to his Christian life in Philippians 1:21, "to die is *gain.*" Sometimes we are tempted to put our confidence in these things because of what appears to

be profitable in so doing. Others think well of you, and they give one a sense of security that you are doing all the right kind of things.

2. As to the *way* he dealt with them—"those things I have counted as loss for the sake of Christ."

a. In his *mind*—"counted"—the word means "to think." He made a mental decision, and that's where the battle rages. You must make up your mind about the value of these "things" or you will never have joy in your life! The aorist tense of this verb suggests it was a definite decision—a moment at which he refused to put value on these things any longer.

b. In his *motivation*—"for the sake of Christ." It was on account of, or because of, Jesus Christ that Paul could make this decision. He compared all of these things with Jesus! To him, they were "loss" (*dzemian*). The word is used also in I Corinthians 3:15 and in II Corinthians 5:10 in reference to the judgment seat of Christ. The word carries the idea of "forfeiting." He laid it all aside. What he experienced in Christ was far better! A complete righteousness provided by the all-sufficient, substitutionary death of Jesus Christ! To know Jesus was worth more than all the religious heritage of the past!

Do you want to have joy today? Then forget the achievements of the past and your many religious activities and service. Look to Jesus and realize again that "things" are not to be compared with *Him*!

STUDY QUESTIONS

1. Explain the meaning of "dogs, evil workers, and false circumcision."
2. How do you recognize the "true circumcision"?
3. What things do you learn for your own life from this passage?

✛✛✛

Your Aims in the Light of God's Plans

✛✛✛

THE CHAPTER OUTLINED:

I. **As to Your Recognition of Values**
   A. Seen in Paul's evaluation
   B. Seen in the excellency of knowing Christ
   C. Seen in Paul's actual experience
   D. Seen in Paul's expectation

II. **As to Your Righteousness**
   A. A description of the wrong kind of righteousness
   B. A definition of the right kind of righteousness

III. **As to Your Response to God**
   A. In acknowledging Christ
   B. In attaining the resurrection of the dead
   C. In achieving God's will for your life
   D. In arriving at the goal

SUGGESTED BACKGROUND DEVOTIONAL READING

Monday—Lord of All (Col. 1:15-19)

Tuesday—Everything in Jesus (Col. 2:1-10)

Wednesday—God's Righteousness (Rom. 3:21-31)

Thursday—The Resurrection (I Cor. 15:12-22)

Friday—Reaching for the Goal (Rom. 8:18-25)

Saturday—The Upward Call (I Thess. 4:13-18)

Sunday—The Final Goal (Rev. 21:1-7)

If you can discover what goals or aims a person has in life, you can learn much about that person. The objectives we have in what we do are often the explanation of why we are doing what we are doing. Many believers fail to experience continual joy in their lives because they do not have the right aims or goals. As we learned in the last chapter, we must forget the past and all of its accomplishments and move on to what lies before us. In this section of the book, Paul deals with his basic motivations and objectives in life. We are finding out what makes him "tick." If the purpose of our lives is to be controlled by Jesus Christ, it must include our aims or goals.

> More than that, I count all things to be loss in view of the surpassing value of knowing Christ Jesus my Lord, for whom I have suffered the loss of all things, and count them but rubbish in order that I may gain Christ, and may be found in Him, not having a righteousness of my own derived from the Law, but that which is through faith in Christ, the righteousness which comes from God on the basis of faith, that I may know Him, and the power of His resurrection and the fellowship of His sufferings, being conformed to His death; in order that I may attain to the resurrection from among the dead. Not that I have already obtained it, or have already become perfect, but I press on in order that I may lay hold of that for which also I was laid hold of by Christ Jesus. Brethren, I do not regard myself as having laid hold of it yet; but one thing I do: forgetting what lies behind and reaching forward to what lies ahead. I press on toward the goal for the prize of the upward call of God in Christ Jesus (Phil. 3:8-14).

I. AS TO YOUR RECOGNITION OF VALUES — 3:8

Verse 7 says, "But whatever things were gain to me, those things I have counted as loss for the sake of Christ." Then, in verse 8, he expands on this by saying that he counts "all things" to be loss and like rubbish when compared with the knowledge of Jesus Christ. He doesn't want any of us to miss the point. One could conclude that the things he mentioned in verses 1 to 7 were easy to give up or they were not worth much, at least to some people. Paul emphasizes that "all things" are to be counted as "loss" when compared with the knowledge of Jesus Christ.

A. Seen in Paul's EVALUATION—"I count all things to be loss . . . and count them but rubbish."

To "count" is to make a mental decision in regard to the values in life. The word means "to lead the way" and comes to mean "to lead before the mind." The thing that is leading the way in which Paul was thinking was the knowledge of Christ. The verb "to count" is present tense meaning that it was a continual habit of Paul to be counting things of no value when compared with the knowledge of Jesus Christ. It was not only a comparison he was making, but he tells us that these "things" were also counted as "rubbish," and "loss." The word "rubbish" (*skubala*) is derived from the word meaning "thrown to dogs." The Judaizers (teachers insisting on circumcision for Gentile converts) counted Gentiles without circumcision as "dogs" and those who were not sitting at the banquet table as it were, but only licking up the crumbs. Paul reverses the image and counts Judaistic ordinances and religious activities as "thrown to dogs." The only way you can understand this is when you understand the greatness of knowing Jesus Christ personally. All the Scriptures speak of Him! All the ceremonies and practices of the Old Testament are types and symbols pointing to Jesus Christ!

B. Seen in the EXCELLENCY of knowing Christ—"in view of the surpassing value of knowing Christ Jesus my Lord."

The words "in view of" mean "because of" or "on account of." This tells us the immediate reason or cause behind Paul's statement that he "counted all things to be loss." The words "surpassing value" mean "to hold over or above." In chapter 2, verse 3, it is translated, "more important than." It's also used in chapter 4, verse 7, when Paul speaks of the peace of God "which *surpasses* all comprehension." In I Peter 2:13, the word is translated "the one in authority," to which we are to submit (same idea in Rom. 13:1—"governing"). The idea of this choice word is that the knowledge of Christ when "held over" us (or all things) as the most important thing in life will cause us to count all things but loss and rubbish. Our recognition of values in this life is definitely related to how important the knowledge of Christ is to us. Paul also reveals somewhat of the controlling influence of this in his life when he calls it "knowing Christ Jesus, the Lord of me." The construction emphasizes that the Lord of his life was Jesus. It is not simply a title for Christ in this passage, like "Lord Jesus Christ," but the emphasis is on Paul's submission to the Lordship of Jesus Christ in his own life. Can you say that the knowledge of Christ Jesus, your Lord, is the most important thing in your life?

C. Seen in Paul's actual EXPERIENCE—"for whom I have suffered the loss of all things."

It was "because of" Christ Jesus that he had suffered the loss of all things. It is not merely the knowledge itself about Christ that changes your value system, but Christ Himself! Paul did not "suffer loss" because of the knowledge he gained, but because of Jesus Christ! "All things" were a part of his suffering loss. The statement is an expansion upon his previous one when he said "I have counted all things to be loss." Now, it is, "I have suffered the loss of all things." It is one thing to "count" or "mentally decide" that all things are of no value in relation to knowing Christ, but it is quite another thing to suffer loss of all these things. Not only did he suffer loss of these things, but because of his commitment to Christ he also suffered!

D. Seen in Paul's EXPECTATION—"that I may gain Christ, and may be found in Him."

This reminds us of Philippians 1:21—"to die is gain." When we speak of "finding" Christ, we usually are talking about someone being converted or becoming a Christian. Is Paul saying that he had not as yet "gained" or "found" Christ? Does this statement indicate that you cannot know whether you are saved or not? Absolutely not! Paul knew quite well that he was a Christian and that he was saved! The expression "be found in Him" and "gain" seem to point to the second coming of Christ (cf. II Peter 3:14) or at least our going to be with Christ at death (cf. Phil. 1:21-23).

II. AS TO YOUR RIGHTEOUSNESS — 3:9

> . . . not having a righteousness of my own derived from the Law, but that which is through faith in Christ, the righteousness which comes from God on the basis of faith.

The second thing that is a part of your "aims" in life deals with your standard of righteousness. You can tell much of what a person is like by what he follows as a standard of righteousness. There are many good people (from a human point of view) in this world who appear to be "Christian" in their actions and words, but who are blind to true righteousness as found in Jesus Christ alone. Jesus said in Matthew 5:20, "For I say to you, that unless your righteousness surpasses that of the scribes and Pharisees, you shall not enter the kingdom of heaven." Obviously, it is not enough to have a standard of righteousness, but rather, the right kind of righteousness! As a Pharisee, Paul had a standard of righteousness which he said in verse 6 was "in the Law" and that he personally was "found blameless."

A. A DESCRIPTION of the wrong kind of righteousness—"not having a righteousness of my own derived from the Law."

There are two things about this statement that show us that Paul's righteousness was the wrong kind. One deals with the words "derived from the Law" which is contrasted with the words "but that which is through faith in Christ." Galatians 3:24 says: "Therefore the Law has become our tutor to lead us to Christ, that we may be justified by faith." Romans 10:4 says: "For Christ is the end of the law for righteousness to everyone who believes." One thing is clear from the teaching of the Bible and that is that one is not saved by the deeds of the law (Rom. 3:28; Gal. 2:16). The Pharisee was trusting in an outward observance of what the law taught and required, but failing to see the need of inward repentance and faith.

The second thing about this statement that shows us that it was a wrong kind of righteousness is the phrase "of my own." It was not Christ's righteousness that Paul had, but his own. Romans 10:3 says of the Jews: "For not knowing about God's righteousness, and seeking to establish their own, they did not subject themselves to the righteousness of God." You may be very proud and confident about the standard of righteousness which you have designed or which you feel is the right kind, but apart from Christ, there is no true righteousness available to any man!

B. A DEFINITION of the right kind of righteousness—"but that which is through faith in Christ, the righteousness which comes from God on the basis of faith."

Three things are taught here about the right kind of righteousness.

1. The *channel* of it—"through faith in Christ." The means by which this righteousness is available or comes to you is faith in Christ, not in yourself or in some external observance or ritual.

2. The *source* of it—"which comes from God." God is the one out of whom righteousness comes. If it is derived from any other source it is the wrong kind.

3. The *basis* of it—"on the basis of faith." God's righteousness is based upon faith alone. You are to believe what Christ has already done for you, not in what you can do for Him!

III. AS TO YOUR RESPONSE TO GOD — 3:10-14

In addition to a recognition of values and an understanding of God's righteousness, the third area affecting your aims and goals in life is the matter of your response to God. We will examine this response in four ways:

A. In ACKNOWLEDGING Christ – 3:10

B. In ATTAINING the resurrection of the dead – 3:11

C. In ACHIEVING God's will for your life – 3:12-13

D. In ARRIVING at the goal – 3:14

Paul has told us that the most important thing in his life is the knowledge of Jesus Christ. He now expands on that and shows us what is involved in this "surpassing knowledge" or "surpassing value of knowledge" as it relates to the Person of Jesus Christ our Lord.

A. In ACKNOWLEDGING Christ – 3:10–". . . that I may know Him, and the power of His resurrection and the fellowship of His sufferings, being conformed to His death."

This is the key verse of chapter 3 and of our third principle of joy–"the purpose of your life must be controlled by Jesus Christ." You might say that this verse is the "heart and soul" of having joy in your life!

1. As to His *Person*–"that I may know Him." Go back to verse 8–"the surpassing value of knowing Christ Jesus my Lord." Paul is referring to his previous statement and stating it very simply but wonderfully–"to know *Him.*" That's what it's all about! Joy in the Christian life is Jesus! The great aim and goal of our lives should be to know *Him!* He is the center of everything! Knowing Him makes everything seem worthwhile and all other things of no importance by comparison!

2. As to His *power*–"and the power of His resurrection." Paul refers to the "power" of the resurrection in his epistle to the Ephesians in chapter 1, verses 19-20:

> . . . and what is the surpassing greatness of *His power* toward us who believe. These are in accordance with the working of the strength of His might which He brought about in Christ, *when He raised Him from the dead,* and seated Him at His right hand in the heavenly places.

The believer may know the "power of His resurrection" in three basic ways:

a. By way of *position*–Ephesians 2:6 says, "and raised us up with Him, and seated us with Him in the heavenly places, in Christ Jesus." When we become believers, we are raised up with Christ and seated with Him. That is our position in Christ. We know the power of His resurrection when we receive new life in Christ.

b. By way of *practice*–Romans 6:4 says, "Therefore we have been buried with Him through baptism into death, in order that as Christ was raised from the dead through the glory of the Father, so we too might walk in newness of life." To "walk in newness of life" is possible only because of the resurrection of Jesus Christ. That refers to our practice or how we "walk."

c. By way of *prospect*—I Thessalonians 4:16-17 says, "For the Lord Himself will descend from heaven with a shout, with the voice of the archangel, and with the trumpet of God; and the dead in Christ shall rise first. Then we who are alive and remain shall be caught up together with them in the clouds to meet the Lord in the air, and thus we shall always be with the Lord." Because Jesus arose from the dead, we also shall rise from the dead.

3. As to *participation* in His sufferings—"and the fellowship of His sufferings." The word "fellowship" refers to that which we share in common (*koinonian*). The word for "sufferings" is the common one used for the sufferings of Christ during his trial and crucifixion. In some sense, we participate in His sufferings. We are recipients of the blessings that result from His sufferings, and in that sense we "share" or "fellowship" with Christ. However, as we examine the testimony of Paul, we discover that he suffered because of his faith in Christ; and in that sense, he fellowshipped with Christ in His sufferings. I Peter 2:21 says, "For you have been called for this purpose, since Christ also suffered for you, leaving you an example for you *to follow in His steps.*" To this passage, Peter adds in I Peter 4:12-14:

> Beloved, do not be surprised at the fiery ordeal among you, which comes upon you for your testing, as though some strange thing were happening to you; but to the degree that you *share the sufferings of Christ,* keep on rejoicing; so that also at the revelation of His glory, you may rejoice with exultation. If you are reviled for the name of Christ, you are blessed, because the Spirit of glory and of God rests upon you.

4. As to the *purpose* of His death—"being conformed to His death." To be "conformed" carries the idea of essential change involving inward nature rather than outward appearance. Some believe that Paul is referring to the kind of humility that led Christ to the cross. The argument here is the same as Philippians 2:5-8. But, when we look at this statement in the light of the verse that follows dealing with the resurrection, it seems that the emphasis is more upon the salvation that Paul had because of what Christ had done at the cross. He then would be stressing the results of Christ's death in his life as they would guarantee his own resurrection from the dead. The present tense of the word "conformed" indicates a continual process whereby the believer experiences the effects of Christ's

death in his life. The word "conformed" also has the preposition "with" attached to it referring to Jesus Christ. Our identification with Him is the issue. Just as a caterpillar is experiencing a process of metamorphosis which is unseen to the outside observer but will one day result in its becoming a butterfly, so we also are undergoing a metamorphosis. The "butterfly" part of this process will not happen until the resurrection or the second coming of Christ. While we live in a "caterpillar shell," our true nature is that of a butterfly. The moment we are saved, we receive a new nature, and at the second coming of Christ we shall be outwardly what we are now inwardly. The process of conformity is based upon what Jesus did at the cross, and His death guarantees our future resurrection and transformation.

B. In ATTAINING the resurrection of the dead — 3:11—". . . in order that I may attain to the resurrection from among the dead."

The words "in order that" come from the word "if" and the word indicating "manner." The idea is "If somehow . . . ." Does this mean that Paul did not know whether or not he would be resurrected? It is not suggesting probability or doubt. It emphasizes the fact that it is going to happen. Paul expected to participate in this resurrection. There was no doubt about that.

1. The *manner* in which it is described—"I may attain." The word "attain" means "to reach" or "to arrive at." Ephesians 4:13 says: "until we all *attain* to the unity of the faith, and of the knowledge of the Son of God, to a mature man, to the measure of the stature which belongs to the fulness of Christ." The idea of "attain" is to arrive at the goal of maturity. Acts 26:7 says: "the promise to which our twelve tribes hope to *attain*, as they earnestly serve God night and day." There was no doubt about God fulfilling His promise. The 12 tribes were hoping to reach that fulfillment. They were relying and trusting upon the promise of God. When Paul says in Philippians 3:11 that he wanted to "attain" the resurrection of the dead, he simply meant that he expected to reach that goal.

2. The *meaning* of the resurrection. The Greek words here are very important. All people will experience a resurrection. Paul is referring to a particular resurrection. The word "resurrection" combines the normal word with the preposition meaning "out of." The last phrase "from among the dead" means literally, "the one out of the dead." From out of all the dead, Paul wanted to be a part of the first resurrection, which would separate him from the wicked dead who will be resurrected to stand before

the Great White Throne Judgment of God (Rev. 20:11-15). The first resurrection occurs 1,000 years or more before that resurrection of the wicked dead (Rev. 20:4-6).

The translation of verse 11 might go something like this: "If, and it is certain I will, by any means possible, I might reach unto the resurrection, the one out from among the dead (wicked dead)." This was the great desire and goal of the Apostle Paul.

C. In ACHIEVING God's will for your life – 3:12-13.

> Not that I have already obtained it, or have already become perfect, but I press on in order that I may lay hold of that for which also I was laid hold of by Christ Jesus. Brethren, I do not regard myself as having laid hold of it yet; but one thing I do: forgetting what lies behind and reaching forward to what lies ahead.

Verse 15 begins, "Let us therefore, as many as are perfect, have this attitude." The perfection that Paul is speaking about is a maturity in the Christian life that sees that we have not arrived yet at the final goal. It is a mark of maturity to understand that we have not arrived at perfection. It almost sounds like a contradiction. To be perfect we must understand that we are not perfect! When you see that Paul is dealing with mature attitudes, it helps to explain what he means in these verses. Some people reveal their immaturity by thinking that they have arrived spiritually at the final goal of absolute perfection. Our position in Christ is perfect, but our present state will not be completed until the resurrection. You are mature ("perfect") if you understand that absolute perfection is still in the future at the resurrection.

1. *Recognizing* your present state–"Not that I have already obtained it, or have already become perfect." The word "obtained" is the simple word "to receive." The simple point is that in this present state of our lives as believers we have not as yet arrived at the final goal. We have not received the wonderful promise of a resurrected and changed body. The words "have already become perfect" are in the perfect tense which would indicate the finality of perfection. We haven't come to that point yet. It's still future.

2. *Resolving* to press on to maturity–"but I press on in order that I may lay hold of that for which also I was laid hold of by Christ Jesus."

a. The *motive* he had–"I press on in order that I may lay hold of." This maturity in Christ was a motivating factor in Paul's life that kept him going. Christ saved him for a purpose which He wanted to fulfill. In Acts

9:15-16 we learn of that purpose.

> But the Lord said to him [Ananias], "Go, for he is a chosen instrument of Mine, to bear My name before the Gentiles and kings and the sons of Israel; for I will show him how much he must suffer for My name's sake."

b. The *meaning* of what he was seeking—"that for which also I was laid hold of by Christ Jesus." It was not simply the purpose that Christ had for Paul during his lifetime that was involved in this statement. It was Christ's eternal purpose in calling Paul to Himself. Paul was looking forward to the day when he would be with Christ and the process which God had begun in him would be finished and complete. Paul kept on in his Christian life, faithful to Christ, knowing that one day he would arrive at the goal which was the original purpose of Christ when Paul became a Christian. It is the same goal or aim that every believer ought to have—to be with Christ in resurrected bodies forever!

3. *Realizing* what you have accomplished in this pursuit—"Brethren, I do not regard myself as having laid hold of it yet." His job was not yet done. He knew that God had more work for him to do on this earth and that it was needful for him to remain in the flesh in order to minister to them (Phil. 1:21-24). We see a change in his words when he wrote the Book of II Timothy. In chapter 4, verses 6-8 we read:

> For I am already being poured out as a drink offering, and the time of my departure has come. I have fought the good fight, I have finished the course, I have kept the faith; in the future there is laid up for me the crown of righteousness, which the Lord, the righteous Judge, will award to me on that day; and not only to me, but also to all who have loved His appearing.

Here it seems that Paul knew that the end was near, and that the goal of his life was almost realized.

4. *Reaching* forward to what lies ahead—"but one thing I do: forgetting what lies behind and reaching forward to what lies ahead." There is a great principle taught here in terms of achieving God's will for your life. Too many people are living in the past instead of forgetting what lies behind. The word "forgetting" means to "neglect" or "forget" and is used in several interesting passages. In a negative way, God never forgets the sparrows (Luke 12:6), or the work of His saints (Heb. 6:10). Believers are not to forget what they see in the mirror of God's Word (James 1:24). In our passage in Philippians, Paul tells us to forget what lies behind. In Luke 9:62 Jesus said: "No one, after putting his hand to the plow and looking

live for future.

back, is fit for the kingdom of God." The word "back" is the same word translated "behind" in our verse. In terms of discipleship, we are not to look to that which is behind, but rather press forward to that which is before us. It is a sickness all too prevalent among believers to look to the accomplishments of the past rather than concentrate on working in the present. Forget that which is behind! All the blessings, the trials, the achievements, the sins . . . forget them all!

Paul then tells us to reach forward to what lies ahead. The word means "to stretch oneself toward." Keep on stretching yourself toward the right goal! It is also in the middle voice indicating you are to do this yourself. Stretch yourself!

There is the tragic story of Lot's wife who instead of looking to that which was ahead, looked back to Sodom and was changed into a pillar of salt. She illustrates the tragic truth that you can take some Christians out of the world, but you cannot take the world out of them! On the other hand, we learn the story of Elisha in I Kings 19:19-21 who left all to follow Elijah. Elisha's great desire was to be a man of God and when given the opportunity, he requested a double portion of God's power upon his life. Are we forgetting what lies behind, and pressing forward to what lies ahead? Our aims as believers are extremely important in controlling what we do and say and as to how effective we are.

D. In ARRIVING at the goal – 3:14–"I press on toward the goal for the prize of the upward call of God in Christ Jesus."

The goal or aim we have is the important issue in this section of Scripture.

1. The *dedication* we should have–"I press on toward the goal." The word "press" means to pursue a thing continually. The words "toward the goal" literally mean "according to watching." The word is the basis for our word "scope." It means to fix the eye on an object or mark. Paul reveals his utter dedication to God's purposes in his life when he informs us that he is constantly pursuing and fixing his eye on a particular mark or goal.

2. The *definition* of the goal–"for the prize of the upward call of God in Christ Jesus." The word for "prize" is from the root "to umpire" and the verb "to decide." The "prize" is the result of the judge's or umpire's decision. The identity of this "prize" is described as being the "upward" calling of God in Christ Jesus. Some believe that this is a reference to the Rapture of the Church when Christ will call home or "up" His saints. While that event is certainly going to happen (I Thess. 4:16-17), it would

appear that the primary emphasis here is on the ultimate goal of the believer which is to be with Christ forever. It is the culmination of that for which he was called by God. Death is not the goal—meeting Christ is! To be with Him has been a continual emphasis of Paul in this book. The prize is the above calling of God—the one that is described in Hebrews 3:1 as the "heavenly calling." It is no wonder that Paul had the joy of the Lord! He was looking forward to being with Christ in heaven. Are you?

STUDY QUESTIONS:

1. What was the excellency of knowing Jesus Christ compared with in this passage?

2. How would you describe the right kind of righteousness?

3. In what sense do believers know the power of His resurrection?

4. What does it mean to be "perfect"?

10 PHILIPPIANS 3:15-21

++

Your Agreement With God's Pattern for You

++

THE CHAPTER OUTLINED:

    I. In Following the Proper Examples
        A. As to our attitudes
        B. As to our attainment
        C. As to our acceptance of Paul's example

    II. In Forsaking the Enemies of the Cross
        A. Their conduct
        B. The characteristics of these enemies

    III. In Fixing Your Eyes upon the Future
        A. On the place where our citizenship is
        B. On the person we are anticipating
        C. On the promise of a changed body

SUGGESTED BACKGROUND DEVOTIONAL READING

Monday—Following Good Examples (I Thess. 1:1-10)

Tuesday—Follow the Leaders (Heb. 13:7-17)

Wednesday—Don't Follow the Wrong Person (II Thess. 3:6-15)

Thursday—Don't Be Foolish (Gal. 3:1-9)

Friday—No Other Gospel (Gal. 1:6-10)

Saturday—A Changed Body (I Cor. 15:35-49)

Sunday—Our Final Home (Rev. 21:9-27)

The connection of this portion of the book with the previous sections is found in the word "therefore" of verse 15. The theme of joy in this book has a constant sub-theme dealing with unity. There seems to be a lack of unity in this local church and as a result, a lack of maturity and common goals and interests. Chapter 2 reminded us that the believers need unity with one another, and the early verses of chapter 4 will emphasize the same thing. Our present portion of Scripture is emphasizing the need of maturity in three areas:

I. In FOLLOWING the proper examples – 3:15-17

II. In FORSAKING the enemies of the cross – 3:18-19

III. In FIXING our eyes upon the future – 3:20-21

God's pattern for you is maturity, and Paul is exhorting the believers in Philippi to bring their lives into complete agreement and harmony with God's pattern of maturity.

> Let us therefore, as many as are perfect, have this attitude; and if in anything you have a different attitude, God will reveal that also to you; however, let us keep living by that same standard to which we have attained. Brethren, join in following my example, and observe those who walk according to the pattern you have in us. For many walk, of whom I often told you, and now tell you even weeping, that they are enemies of the cross of Christ, whose end is destruction, whose god is their appetite, and whose glory is in their shame, who set their minds on earthly things. For our citizenship is in heaven, from which also we eagerly wait for a Savior, the Lord Jesus Christ; who will transform the body of our humble state into conformity with the body of His glory, by the exertion of the power that He has even to subject all things to Himself.

I. IN FOLLOWING THE PROPER EXAMPLES – 3:15-17

It is easy to follow the wrong thing. The world is filled with people who do this. Paul motivated people to follow his example because he was following the Lord. His own goals in life reflect that he was living for Jesus Christ alone! When this is true of us, we are in position to affect the lives of others.

A. As to our ATTITUDES – 3:15.

> Let us therefore, as many as are perfect, have this attitude; and if in anything you have a different attitude, God will reveal that also to you.

1. Based on our *maturity*—"as many as are perfect, have this attitude." The word "perfect" does not mean "without sin," but rather indicates

maturity or completeness. It would refer to that which is mature in the context. The "therefore" connects it with the preceding verses. Maturity is described by Paul as forgetting the things which are behind, and reaching forth unto the things ahead. If anyone is mature in that, he is exhorted to be minding this matter. We are to fix our minds upon the kind of maturity that does not trust in past achievements, but counts all as loss in order to gain Christ.

2. Based on the *means* God uses to reveal proper attitudes—"and if in anything you have a different attitude, God will reveal that also to you." The word "different" (*heteros*) is an adverb referring to "another of a different kind." The point is that if our mental attitude is going another way than this kind of maturity, we are on the wrong track and are following the wrong example. Paul tells us that God will reveal this to us. He does not say how God will do this, but our experiences as believers show us that God wants us to be mature more than we want to be. He will use various means to keep us thinking the right way. His loving discipline often reveals which path is correct.

Maturity in our attitudes is so very important. You can lose your joy in the Lord so quickly by following the wrong thing, and by concentrating on wrong goals and objectives in your life.

B. As to our ATTAINMENT – 3:16.

> However, let us keep living by that same standard to which we have attained.

The verse begins with an adverb which unfolds what has just preceded. The word "however" or "nevertheless" expresses the idea. If we want to attain to the mature attitudes mentioned in the previous verse, we must follow the instruction of this verse. The word "attained" means "to come to; arrive at; reach, and so on." Paul uses it in I Thessalonians 4:15 where the ones living at the time of Christ's coming will not "precede" those who have died in Christ in terms of being caught up to meet the Lord in the air. The point to which we have come in our maturity is the point at which we are exhorted to "keep living by that same standard." The King James Version carries two lines of thought, that of "walking" and that of "minding." The New American Standard Bible follows what appears to be better manuscript evidence which carries only the one thought of "walking" or "living." The verb indicates the idea of walking step by step. It refers to proceeding "in a row," or to "go in order." It's a very descriptive word in terms of our maturity—a step at a time! We get the word "Stoic" from this word. The Stoic was a person who was strict in morals, but followed rules and regulations step by step.

To summarize, the idea would be that we are to continue a step-by-step pattern in accordance with the maturity we have already seen developed in our lives, and which we see in the life of Paul.

C. As to our ACCEPTANCE of Paul's example — 3:17.

Brethren, join in following my example, and observe those who walk according to the pattern you have in us.

1. The basic *instruction.*

a. As to the *way* we are to follow him—"join in following my example." Literally it reads, "Continually become imitators of me." The words "following my example" use a word whose root is used in a good sense in the Scripture (I Cor. 4:16; 11:1; Eph. 5:1; I Thess. 1:6; 2:14; II Thess. 3:7, 9; Heb. 6:12; 13:7; and III John 11). The preposition "with" is combined with the word for "mimic." Paul is exhorting us to mimic him, walking step by step alongside of his life. That's quite a statement! The only way a man can do this is if he himself is following the Lord!

b. As to the *watching* of others—"and observe those who walk." The word "observe" means to be constantly looking or observing. We get our English word "scope" from this word. In the Greek text there is a little word inserted here which means "in such a manner." The idea is that we are to continually observe the ones who are constantly walking in such a manner as to reflect the proper pattern of maturity. It is good to remember this is our desire to have joy in our Christian walk. Follow good examples! Associate with people who will encourage your maturity in Christ!

2. The basic *illustration*—"according to the pattern you have in us." We might translate this phrase, "just as you are having us, a pattern." It is not simply a pattern "in us," but "us" as the pattern! The word "pattern" comes from the root word meaning "to strike." The idea is that of a blow that leaves an impression or mark, like the impress of a stamp. Frequently this word is combined with the preposition meaning "under" and refers to a pattern under from which you could trace your life. Paul includes others with himself in this "pattern." New believers especially should not hesitate in following the examples of their spiritual leaders. It will bring direction and maturity into their lives and the joy of the Lord. We, of course, should keep our eyes on the Lord instead of people. However, we should follow the godly patterns that are being lived for the Lord.

II. IN FORSAKING THE ENEMIES OF THE CROSS — 3:18-19

> For many walk, of whom I often told you, and now tell you even weeping, that they are enemies of the cross of Christ, whose end is destruction, whose god is their appetite, and whose glory is in their shame, who set their minds on earthly things.

Not only must we follow the proper examples, but we must also forsake those people who would hinder our growth and maturity in the Lord. Paul is primarily referring to the people he mentioned earlier in this chapter—the Judaizers. They were the teachers who insisted on outward religious observance and ritual performance of circumcision for all the Gentile believers. Paul calls them "enemies of the cross."

A. Their CONDUCT — 3:18.

1. Paul's *reminder* of their conduct—"For many walk, of whom I often told you." The word "many" suggests that it was not an isolated incident or problem that he was referring to, but it was widespread. The word "walk" is in the present tense meaning that many were continually walking in this manner. It was a constant practice. The words "of whom I often told you" show us that Paul was continually warning them about this. The word "often" is an adverb indicating "frequently." We can learn a principle from this that in addition to teaching new converts how to grow in maturity, we must also warn them of those who will deceive them and get them off the right track.

2. Paul's *reaction* to their conduct—"and now tell you even weeping." The word "weeping" indicates a loud expression of grief like mourning for the dead (cf. John 11:31, 33). Paul did not tell them of these false teachers because it brought him much joy. On the contrary, he said this with a broken heart. It was like the loss of a loved one.

3. Their *resistance* to the true Gospel—"they are enemies of the cross of Christ." They lost sight of the finality of Christ's death on the cross ("It is finished!"). He set men free and paid for all the righteous demands of the law. To impose Mosaic restrictions upon these Gentile believers made them "enemies of the cross of Christ." These are strong words, but they reveal how important is the issue of Christ's death as both a substitution for all our sins, as well as a satisfaction of the demands of God's law. Romans 10:4 tells us, "For Christ is the end of the law for righteousness to everyone who believes."

B. The CHARACTERISTICS of these enemies — 3:19.

After stating that they are "enemies," Paul now proceeds to prove why he said this. He gives us four lines of proof.

1. As to their *destruction*—"whose end is destruction." The word "destruction" is not a mild word. It appears that Paul is indicating that those whose trust is in outward ceremonies and works are heading for eternal destruction. If they are not trusting in the finished work of Christ on the cross, then there is no hope for them!

2. As to their *dependence*—"whose god is their appetite." Now at first glance you might think that this statement is referring to those whose sensual appetites were out of control. However, that does not fit these people. They were strict in outward observance of the law. The word "appetite" or "belly" (KJV) comes from the word meaning "womb." The root idea is that of "hollow." It could refer to their trust in and belief in the womb! Their god was their genealogy—to be in the true line! They thought that as long as you were a Jew and could prove your lineage, that was enough to save you. But the Bible teaches that the true sons of Abraham are those who are of faith (Rom. 4:11-12). It is not enough to be circumcised. That was only an outward sign of inward faith in God's promise. These "enemies" were depending upon their descent and ancestry for their eternal salvation. They are like many people today who believe they are Christians simply because their father and mother were Christians. It is not enough to be born into a Christian home. That does not save you! Only Christ can save you!

3. As to their *defilement*—"whose glory is in their shame." There are two basic issues of the word "shame":

(1) To have a feeling or sense of shame which prevents you from doing something.

(2) The sense of shame arising from something you've already done.

The point of this phrase is that the realm or sphere of that which they glory in (namely—outward ceremonies, physical descent, rite of circumcision, and so forth), is their shame. It should give them a sense of shame from trusting in the wrong thing. "Shame" is usually associated with immoral living. Here the defilement is that which they glory or trust in!

4. As to their *desires*—"who set their minds on earthly things." A very common term in this Book of Philippians is the verb "to mind." Here it is referring to the ones who are continually minding the things upon the earth. Much of our problem can be attributed to this kind of mental concentration. Instead of fixing our mental attention on "things above" (Col. 3:1-4) we are concentrating on earthly things. The "things on earth"

in this context would refer to man's deeds and works—the outward religious observance and practices.

It is no wonder that Paul calls these people the "enemies of the cross of Christ." Their number is legion. Everywhere you turn there is someone else trying to get believers (especially new ones!) to follow a legalistic pattern rather than trusting in the work of Christ alone! We all need to remember the centrality of the cross in terms of salvation and Christian life and growth.

III. IN FIXING YOUR EYES UPON THE FUTURE — 3:20-21

> For our citizenship is in heaven, from which also we eagerly wait for a Savior, the Lord Jesus Christ; who will transform the body of our humble state into conformity with the body of His glory, by the exertion of the power that He has even to subject all things to Himself.

What glorious words these are! Talk about having joy! God's pattern for our lives is not simply in this life, but will culminate in a glorious future! A key to having the joy of the Lord and real maturity in your life is your ability to fix your mind upon the "things above," and the wonderful future God has prepared for you and me. Some people think that this is a cop out on responsibilities down here on earth. We often hear people say, "He's so heavenly minded that he's no earthly good!" That statement is obviously not in the Bible, nor is it spiritual in any sense. The Bible teaches that if we are "heavenly minded" we will be of "earthly good." Our failure to "lay up treasures in heaven" is the root of many of our problems. We live only for this life and that is why we are so miserable (cf. I Cor. 15:19). Let's turn our attention now to the glorious future awaiting us and see some of the exciting things we are going to experience. We need to fix our eyes on three main things according to these verses.

A. On the PLACE where our citizenship is — 3:20.

"For our citizenship is in heaven." The word "is" carries an importance in this statement. It is used here to mean to "be existing" at the present time. Our actual citizenship is existing right now in heaven! It is not something we're going to have in the future. We're citizens of heaven right now! Jesus said in John 18:36: "My kingdom is not of this world. If My kingdom were of this world, then My servants would be fighting, that I might not be delivered up to the Jews; but as it is My kingdom is not of this realm." The word "citizenship" comes from the word from which we get our word "politics." Our political affiliation is in heaven! That's very important to remember when we see the problems of politics down here! Let's make sure we are lined up on the right side! The "citizenship" is not simply a ticket to some place, but indicates our homeland, the place where we really belong.

B. On the PERSON we are anticipating — 3:20.

From which also we eagerly wait for a Savior, the Lord Jesus Christ.

Real joy in the Christian life is very much related to our anticipation of the Person of Jesus Christ. In John 14:3, He said, "I will come again, and receive you to Myself; that where I am, there you may be also."

1. The *source* from which He's coming—"from which." These words are referring back to the word "heaven." In Acts 1:11 it says: "And they also said, Men of Galilee, why do you stand looking into the sky? This Jesus, who has been taken up from you into heaven, will come in just the same way as you have watched Him go into heaven." He went into heaven and will come again from heaven. I Thessalonians 4:16 says, "For the Lord Himself will descend from heaven."

2. The *salvation* we are anticipating—"we eagerly wait for a Savior." The words "eagerly wait" come from a combination of three words: "receive" plus "from" plus "out of." We are going to "receive" Him "from" and "out of" heaven. We are anticipating a "Savior." There is no question who it will be, for the text says, "Lord Jesus Christ." In Titus 2:13 we read, "looking for the blessed hope and the appearing of the glory of our great God and Savior, Christ Jesus." Some groups teach that both the Father and the Son will come from heaven. This is an attempt to avoid the obvious point—Christ Jesus is our great God and Savior! In Greek, the words "God" and "Savior" are connected grammatically as equals. The definite article "the" appears before "God" but not before "Savior." Yes, it is Jesus, our God and Savior, whom we are anticipating from heaven! He is coming soon! That anticipation can really affect your joy and happiness in the Lord!

C. On the PROMISE of a changed body — 3:21.

Who will transform the body of our humble state into conformity with the body of His glory, by the exertion of the power that He has even to subject all things to Himself.

This verse contains many fascinating insights into what our transformed state will be like in the future. This can really bring joy into a person's life, especially if he has suffered physically to any degree. Paul wrote in Romans 8:18, "For I consider that the sufferings of this present time are not worthy to be compared with the glory that is to be revealed to us." In verse 23, he calls it "the redemption of our body." In II Corinthians 4:16-18, Paul wrote: "Therefore we do not lose heart, but though our outer man is decaying, yet our inner man is being renewed day by day. For momentary, light affliction is producing for us an eternal weight of glory far beyond all comparison, while we look not at the things which are seen, but at the things which are not seen; for the things which are seen are temporal, but the things which are not seen are eternal." The Word of God is filled with such encouragement! The real joy is not anticipating what tomorrow may bring on earth, but that tomorrow may bring the return of Christ and a transformed body for each believer!

1. The *change* that will occur—"who will transform the body of our humble state into conformity with the body of His glory." There are two basic words used here to describe that change.

a. "Transformed" (*metaschematisei*)—this refers to a change in appearance. We get our words "schizo" and "schizophrenia" from this word. When we use those words we refer to someone who has withdrawn from reality and who manifests two personalities or "split personalities." He has an inward personality and an appearance to others which is different. The preposition in front of this word means "after" and indicates a change in appearance will take place. Does this mean that our bodies will outwardly change in appearance and look exactly like Jesus Christ's body in appearance? The answer to that is no. The reason is that another word would be used to describe that (*suschematidzo*) which means to give the same appearance. We will not look like Jesus Christ, but we will look differently than we look now. The change in appearance involves the character or nature of our bodies. They will be restructured and redesigned so that they will function like the body of Jesus Christ after His resurrection. Our bodies will have abilities and capacities that they do not presently have.

b. "Conformity"—this word means "to change with." It emphasizes inward change. The inward transformation will result in a likeness or sameness with the body of Jesus Christ. The qualities of Christ's body that make it perform as it does will be found in our bodies. Presumably that means that we will not be limited in going through walls as He did or traveling at great speeds and distances throughout the universe. There is no way that we can know exactly what our capacities will be like, but they will be greatly increased from what we know now. The physical properties of our bodies will be changed like Christ's physical body, and our outward appearance will change even though we will not look like Jesus Christ in appearance. I John 3:2-3 puts it, "Beloved, now we are children of God, and it has not appeared as yet that we shall be. We know that, if He should appear, we shall be like Him, because we shall see Him just as He is. And every one who has this hope fixed on Him purifies himself, just as He is pure."

2. The *contrast* in bodies. Christ's body is described as "the body of His glory." Our present body is described as "the body of our humble state." Quite a contrast! We get a glimpse of what His body is like in Matthew 17:1-5, an event which Peter refers to in II Peter 1:16-18. On that mount of transfiguration, they saw His "glory" displayed (cf. John 1:14). Matthew 17:2 says, "and His face shone like the sun, and His garments became as white as light." Our bodies are described as being "lowly" by comparison. But one day, praise God, they are going to be exalted!

3. The *cause* behind all of this—"by the exertion of the power that He has even to subject all things to Himself."

a. The *energy* of Christ—"the exertion of the power that He has." The words "the power that He has" means the power He has in and of Himself. What a statement to the deity of Christ! It is His power that will change our bodies one day!

b. The *extent* of His power—"even to subject all things to Himself." Hebrews 2:8 says, "Thou hast put all things in subjection under His feet. For in subjecting all things to him, He left nothing that is not subject to him. But now we do not yet see all things subjected to him." Christ will rule and reign over "all things." He has tremendous power! That same power to subject everything is the power with which He will resurrect our bodies and transform them!

If you really want joy, then follow the proper examples, forsake the enemies of the cross, and most important of all, fix your eyes upon our glorious future!

STUDY QUESTIONS:

1. What is the example we are to follow?
2. Who are the "enemies of the cross"?
3. Explain how our bodies are going to be changed in the future.

Principles of Joy

+++

PRINCIPLE NO. 4

THE PROVISION OF YOUR LIFE
MUST BE COMPLETE IN CHRIST

Philippians 4:1-23

KEY VERSE: Philippians 4:19—"And my God shall supply all your needs according to His riches in glory in Christ Jesus."

II   PHILIPPIANS 4:1-7

Your Assurance
of God's Peace

THE CHAPTER OUTLINED:

   I. **In Reacting to Others**
      A. The need for steadfastness
      B. The necessity of unity

  II. **In Rejoicing in the Lord**
      A. The pattern of rejoicing that is needed
      B. The place of rejoicing
      C. The priority of rejoicing

 III. **In Relaxing Before Others**
      A. The nature of this relaxing
      B. The nearness of the Lord

 IV. **In Resting in the Lord**
      A. The principle of trust
      B. The prayer with thanksgiving
      C. The peace that controls our lives

SUGGESTED BACKGROUND DEVOTIONAL READING

Monday—Joy and Sorrow (John 16:16-24)

Tuesday—Joy in His Presence (Ps. 16)

Wednesday—Rejoice in the Lord (Ps. 107:1-9)

Thursday—Shout Joyfully to the Lord (Ps. 98)

Friday—His Peace (John 14:25-31)

Saturday—Cast Your Care on Him (I Peter 5:6-11)

Sunday—Peace of God (Rom. 5:1-11)

The wonderful conclusion of chapter 3 is the immediate reason for what the writer says at the beginning of chapter 4. The word "therefore" reminds us of this as it is a word emphasizing result. The result of knowing that our "citizenship" is in heaven and that Jesus Christ is soon to return and that our bodies will be redesigned is "to stand firm in the Lord." When we realize what will soon take place when Jesus returns, it motivates us to have proper relationships with one another and to have personal joy and peace under all of life's circumstances and trials.

> Therefore, my beloved brethren, whom I long to see, my joy and crown, so stand firm in the Lord, my beloved. I urge Euodia and I urge Syntyche to live in harmony in the Lord. Indeed, true comrade, I ask you also to help these women who have shared my struggle in the cause of the gospel, together with Clement also, and the rest of my fellow-workers, whose names are in the book of life. Rejoice in the Lord always; again I will say, rejoice! Let your forbearing spirit be known to all men. The Lord is near. Be anxious for nothing, but in everything by prayer and supplication with thanksgiving let your requests be made known to God. And the peace of God, which surpasses all comprehension, shall guard your hearts and your minds in Christ Jesus (Phil. 4:1-7).

I. IN REACTING TO OTHERS – 4:1-3

Perhaps one of the more difficult areas in which to have God's peace is in our reaction to others. Getting along with people is one of the critical problems of life, whether you are a Christian or a non-Christian. It is even more serious once you become a Christian. The Bible teaches that all believers are "one" in the Lord, and that this has very practical implications in how we treat one another and what we do to meet one another's needs. Any display of disunity is contradictory to what Christ taught us about loving one another. God expects us to get along with one another, forgiving, sharing, bearing each other's burdens, and so forth. The "unity of the Spirit" has been a continual underlying theme of this book. It is a key factor in having joy in your life. If you are not getting along with other believers, it will affect your personal joy in the Lord.

A. The NEED for steadfastness – 4:1.

> Therefore, my beloved brethren whom I long to see, my joy and crown, so stand firm in the Lord, my beloved.

Whenever Paul gets ready to exhort or rebuke the believers, it seems that he always prepares them for it by reminding them of his love for them and his personal concern.

1. The *manner* in which Paul describes them—"my beloved brethren whom I long to see, my joy and crown . . . my beloved."

a. By way of *relationship*—Paul calls them "brothers," for in Christ that is exactly what they were. Two words are chosen by Paul to modify the word "brothers." One is translated "beloved" and the other "whom I long to see," which simply means "longed for ones." Paul loved them dearly and he also longed for them and for their fellowship. These people in Philippi were very close to Paul and they meant a great deal to him. He was saddened to hear of their lack of unity and growth in the Lord, and he wrote this epistle to encourage them and to motivate them toward the joy of the Lord.

b. By way of *reward*—Paul also describes them as his "joy and crown." This tells us how he felt about them and how he viewed his ministry in their lives. He was personally rewarded by the opportunity to lead them to Christ. His priorities are evident here. The "crown" of his life was not worldly fame or great possessions, but rather the people to whom he had ministered the gospel of Christ. It reminds us of his words in I Thessalonians 2:19-20:

> For who is our hope or joy or crown of exultation? Is it not even you,
> in the presence of our Lord Jesus at His coming? For you are our glory
> and joy.

2. The *meaning* of his instruction—"so stand firm in the Lord." This statement could probably be taken as a summary of the entire book, but especially of chapter 3. He warned them of certain false teachers and enemies of the cross. The point is—"don't lose your joy!" To "stand firm in the Lord" would be the key instruction in facing these false teachers and doctrines that attempted to enslave them to the Mosaic law and its ritual of circumcision. The meaning would be to stand firm at the point of facing the false teachers. Others hold that it means "to stand firm" or "persevere," emphasizing a continual "standing firm." It would be a pattern of life.

B. The NECESSITY of unity—4:2-3.

> I urge Euodia and I urge Syntyche to live in harmony in the Lord. Indeed, true comrade, I ask you also to help these women who have shared my struggle in the cause of the gospel, together with Clement also, and the rest of my fellow-workers, whose names are in the book of life.

It is very difficult to have God's peace without the unity of the Spirit. Paul brings up a particular situation in that church that appears to have been shared with him, perhaps by Epaphroditus, or by a recent letter from them.

1. Seen in the *illustration* of two women—4:2. The words "I urge" are often translated "to encourage, comfort, exhort" and literally mean "to call alongside of." The verb is in the present tense meaning that Paul was beseeching or exhorting them repeatedly. The name of the first woman, Euodia, is from two words, one meaning "good" and the other meaning "way" or "journey." Her name means "a good (prosperous) journey." There is probably no direct significance of her name, but one is tempted to apply it in that we cannot possibly have a "good journey" in our Christian life and growth without living in harmony with others. The name of the other woman, Syntyche, is also interesting in that it means "to meet with" or "to come to." In solving their differences, they needed to meet with one another.

2. Seen in the *instruction* Paul gives to them—2:2-3.

a. With reference to the *women*—"to live in harmony in the Lord"—4:2. This phrase means "to be minding the same (thing) in the Lord." It reminds us of his instruction in the early part of chapter 2. The key to unity is in our ability to be thinking the same things with one another.

b. With reference to the *workers*—4:3. The simple instruction is "to help these women."

(1) The *people* involved. There appear to be several people who were being instructed to offer help in this situation. The first is called a "true comrade." The word (*gnesiesudzuge*) comes from a root referring to one who is legitimately born and therefore, genuine, and also from a word meaning "to yoke together." Some hold this to be a proper name—*Synzygus*. The way the verse is constructed causes some to believe that this person, whoever he is, was probably the accepted leader of the church in Philippi in the absence of Epaphroditus. The second person involved is Clement. We know nothing of who this man was, and his name was very common in those times. The question is whether Paul is saying that this "true comrade" is to bring the help to these women along with Clement and the rest of his fellow workers, or whether he is saying that Clement and the rest of his fellow workers shared in the Gospel with these women. It seems that the latter is the best. The main responsibility, therefore, to help these women is put upon the shoulders of the one referred to as "true comrade."

2. The *purpose* involved—"to help these women." The words "to help"

mean "to take hold together with someone." It carries the idea of "assist" and thus, "help." This admonition to "help these women" is based upon two things according to verse 3:

(a) It was based upon the *faithfulness* they displayed in the work of the Gospel. The words "shared my struggle" are a combination of our word "athlete" and the word "with." They were engaged in the original "struggle" of sharing the Gospel in Philippi along with Paul. They supported him in that effort. It was because of this that Paul wanted them to get their problems worked out. They were important people in terms of their ministry, and Paul hated to see them with this difference between one another.

(b) It was based upon the *fact* of their names being in the Book of Life. They were believers and thus, should get their problems worked out. After all, they are going to spend an eternity together. Isn't it sad to see so many believers who cannot get along with one another down here on earth and realize that we are going to be in heaven with one another forever?

II. IN REJOICING IN THE LORD – 4:4

"Rejoice in the Lord always; again I will say, rejoice!" In addition to our reaction to others, another important area in knowing the assurance of God's peace is in our rejoicing in the Lord. This is a wonderful verse and has much to say to all of us!

A. The PATTERN of rejoicing that is needed.

The Greek word (*chairete*) is in the present tense and means, "be constantly rejoicing." And if that wasn't enough, Paul adds the word "always" and makes it really obvious! The key is not rejoicing when things are exciting and "going our way." It is rejoicing all the time! No matter what the circumstances that we are facing! Our whole attitude would radically change if this verse were a daily principle of our lives!

B. The PLACE of rejoicing – "in the Lord."

Too many times we find ourselves rejoicing in the wrong thing or person. The key to this little epistle is not simply "joy," but "joy *in the Lord*." This phrase indicates the sphere or realm in which all this rejoicing is to take place. Every believer can rejoice if it is "in the Lord," and not in himself or his circumstances.

C. The PRIORITY of rejoicing – "again I will say rejoice!"

Paul doesn't want us to miss the point. It bears repeating—"again." When he repeats it he again uses the present tense—"be constantly rejoicing," that is, "make it the habit of your life."

III.   IN RELAXING BEFORE OTHERS — 4:5

Let your forbearing spirit be known to all men. The Lord is near.

A. The NATURE of this relaxing—"Let your forbearing spirit be known to all men."

a. As to its *expression* toward others. What is the meaning of a "forbearing spirit?" It comes to mean that which is "equitable" or "fair." The Greeks use it in the sense of yielding to others. It is a yielding spirit. It is often seen as a gentle spirit which does not insist upon the letter of the law. It does not seek its own way and insist upon its rights. How important this is in terms of having unity and a spirit of love among the believers! It is used in several interesting passages. In I Timothy 3:3 it is one of the qualifications of the pastor. It appears in the general instruction to believers about submission in Titus 3:2. James 3:17 lists it as one of the characteristics of God's wisdom. I Peter 2:18 uses it when referring to masters of servants who are "gentle."

2. As to its *extent*—"be known to all men." It is much easier to demonstrate this "forbearing spirit" to those we like or who show a similar response to us. But Paul tells us to show it to "all men." That is the test! When someone is antagonistic or hostile to us, it is very difficult to "yield" to them.

B. The NEARNESS of the Lord — "The Lord is near."

This appears to be the reason why we should show this "forbearing spirit to all men." There are two basic ways to take this statement. It could refer to the second coming of Christ. Since His coming is near, we are to exercise great care in our attitudes toward each other. Or, it could refer to the fact of the Lord's presence being near to us at all times. The latter seems to be the better view here. The Lord is always with us, reminding us of the need to do what He would do, say what He would say, and react as He would react. His presence is in the midst of the believers. He said, "I will never leave you, nor forsake you" (cf. Heb. 13:5). His presence is also within the believer through the Person of the Holy Spirit. We can draw upon His power in times of need, especially in our reactions before others.

IV.   IN RESTING IN THE LORD — 4:6-7

Be anxious for nothing, but in everything by prayer and supplication

with thanksgiving let your requests be made known to God. And the
peace of God, which surpasses all comprehension, shall guard your
hearts and your minds in Christ Jesus.

What wonderful verses! Believers find great comfort in them and often
quote them in time of need and stress. They are filled with much instruction and blessing. There are three basic thoughts which run through these
verses that affect our assurance of God's peace. One deals with the principle of trust; two, with the prayer of thanksgiving; and three, with the
peace that controls us.

A. The PRINCIPLE of trust — "Be anxious for nothing."

This phrase is difficult to identify with, especially if you are prone to
worry. Probably no verse seems so out of touch with reality than this one.
Is it really possible not to worry about anything at all? Sometimes this
leads one to show a real lack of concern in an effort to prove that he is not
worrying about something or someone. But, let's face it! We all worry at
one time or another. Call it "anxious care" or "deep concern" or whatever
you want—we still worry! It is natural for human beings to do this. And
yet, this phrase is very strong—"for nothing." That means exactly what
you think it means—we are not to worry about any thing—not even one
thing! The key to understanding this is wrapped up in the meaning of "be
anxious." The word means "to be divided" or "distracted." Literally it
carries the idea of drawing in different directions. Jesus used this word
when answering Martha in Luke 10:41: "But the Lord answered and said
to her, 'Martha, Martha, you are *worried* and bothered about so many
things.'" He went on to tell her that the one thing she had left out was
what Mary had chosen and that was to sit at the feet of Jesus and learn.
Now Martha's worry was basically a distraction. She was distracted from
the priority of the moment. She was drawn away from what was the most
important to something that was good and necessary but not needed at the
time, or the most could wait.

It seems to this writer that the meaning of "be anxious for nothing"
refers to the attitude of trust in the life of the believer that accepts all
things as being truly from the Lord and for his good. The basic reason why
we don't have God's peace is because we are not accepting all things as
being from God. We are not trusting God. We are being drawn away from
that principle of trust and now distracted by our circumstances and trials.
Romans 8:28 says: "And we know that God causes all things to work
together for good to those who love God, to those who are called accord-

ing to His purpose." Romans 11:36 tells us: "For from Him and through Him and to Him are all things. To Him be the glory forever, Amen." The Scriptures are clear in teaching us that "all things" truly come from God. Our need is simply to trust Him and know that all will be well. That will bring real and wonderful peace into our hearts.

B. The PRAYER with thanksgiving—"in everything by prayer and supplication with thanksgiving let your requests be made known to God."

It is easy to pray sometimes, especially when you are in trouble or difficulty, but it is not so easy to pray with thanksgiving!

1. The *contrast* of it—"but in everything." One cannot help but notice this in the verse. "Be anxious for *nothing,* but in *everything.*" The word "but" is a word of great contrast. In contrast to one who is distracted from trusting God in all things, learn to pray in every circumstance of life. Now we also learn a principle about what leads to worry or divided attention or distraction from trusting God—it is a lack of prayer. We wait until the last minute to pray. When all else fails, then we say, "Let's pray about it." It would be better to have the habit of prayer in every detail of our lives.

2. The *character* of this prayer. There are four words used here to describe this prayer of which one is the most important in terms of having God's peace in your life.

a. "Prayer"—here is a word that could be translated "worship." It is not a word of demand. We are not encouraged here to demand God to act in our behalf. The basic idea is that of giving thanks toward God. It is a word of praise toward God. Much of our praying is deficient in that so little of it falls into the category of praising God. We are too busy asking for things. We are certainly encouraged to ask for things but not to the exclusion of thanksgiving and praise.

b. "Supplication"—this word emphasizes the matter of urgent need and request. It expresses the kind of prayer we offer when the pressure is on, and when the need is very great and serious. Too often we are not very serious or urgent in our prayer life, and we fail to follow the examples of our Lord in Luke 11 (a friend begs for three loaves of bread at midnight) and Luke 18 (a widow begs the unjust judge for legal protection). In these two incidents our Lord admonishes us to keep on asking and with a degree of urgency. How much do we really want God to answer our prayers?

c. "Requests"—this comes from the simple word "to ask." It is "the askings" that we are encouraged to bring to God. We can ask God for anything and everything. He tells us much about our failure to ask Him, and about how much He, as a loving heavenly Father, wants to give to us.

d. "Thanksgiving"—this obviously is the key word to this verse. The preposition "with" tells us that. All this praying "in everything" must be done "with thanksgiving" if the peace of God is to result. Our failure to thank God for all things that happen is at the root of our lack of peace and joy. It is easy to thank Him for blessings; it is more difficult to thank Him for trials. Don't let anything, no matter how great a trial it is, take your mind away from praying with thanksgiving to God! If you are presently going through some deep waters, or you have recently been submerged in many trials and difficulties, then right now lift up your praise and thanksgiving to God and thank Him for bringing these trials into your life so that you can grow to maturity and have your own ministry increased in the lives of others, and have a greater anticipation of heaven and our future glory (cf. Rom. 8:18-25; II Cor. 1:3-7; 4:16-18; Peter 5:8-10 and many others). You will be so glad that you did, and God's peace will begin to control your mind and heart and fill you with God's joy in all you do and say.

3. The *commitment* to God—"let your requests be made known to God." There is an important principle here about leaving your request with the Lord. So often we let our requests be made known to scores of other believers, instead of taking them to the Lord. Much talk is cheap when it comes to discussing our needs with others. The real test is how much we go to the Lord about these matters. Is our commitment to Him strong? Does it come before anyone else?

C. The PEACE that controls our lives — 4:7.

> And the peace of God, which surpasses all comprehension, shall guard your hearts and your minds in Christ Jesus.

Peace, wonderful peace! People will go to any end to find it! The rich would sometimes give all they have in order to have peace. Rulers would give up their kingdoms in order to have peace. The world is full of trouble, turmoil, strife, and a great lack of peace. There is a point at which we must all begin in order to have peace. Romans 5:1 deals with it when it says: "Therefore having been justified by faith, we have peace with God through our Lord Jesus Christ." We must begin by receiving "peace *with* God." This comes by being justified by faith. A man must be declared righteous by God in order to have peace with God. All believers have this kind of peace the moment they trust in Jesus Christ as their Saviour. After that occurs, we must go on to discover the "peace" that is a part of the fruit of the Spirit (cf. Gal. 5:22) and the quality that controls and stabilizes our minds and hearts.

1. The *greatness* of it—"which surpasses all comprehension." The word "surpasses" means "to hold above." The word "comprehension" is from the root word for "mind," and refers to the ability to perceive. It is to be separated by perception that comes by feeling, however. The peace of God goes beyond the ability of the mind to rationally perceive or understand how it works or functions.

2. The *guarding* it does—"shall guard your hearts and minds in Christ Jesus."

a. The *security* involved—"guard." This word refers to keeping with a military guard. It carries the idea of security and protection by the military. God's peace provides wonderful security to us.

b. The *scope* of what is involved—"your hearts and minds." The word for "minds" would emphasize the individual thoughts of the mind. The ability of the mind to think is being controlled by the peace of God— praise God!

c. The *sphere* in which this happens—"in Christ Jesus." In Christ Jesus we have nothing to fear; outside of Him we have everything to fear. What peace and security we have in knowing Jesus Christ and living in Him!

STUDY QUESTIONS:

1. To what does the phrase "stand firm in the Lord" refer?
2. What did you learn about the phrase "rejoice in the Lord"?
3. What is a "forbearing spirit"?
4. What kind of prayer should be offered by the believer?
5. Explain the meaning of "Be anxious for nothing."

12 PHILIPPIANS 4:8-13

+++

Your Aspirations
Toward Your Priorities

+++

THE CHAPTER OUTLINED:

  I. **As to Your Concentration on Important Things**
     A. A description of what is important
     B. A duty we have toward these things

 II. **As to Your Conduct**
     A. The responsibility we have
     B. The result we can expect

III. **As to Your Contentment**
     A. Seen in Paul's expression of joy
     B. Seen in Paul's experience

 IV. **As to Your Confidence**
     A. The strength involved
     B. The scope of it
     C. The source of it

SUGGESTED BACKGROUND DEVOTIONAL READING

Monday—Think on Jesus (Col. 3:1-4)

Tuesday—Qualities We Should Have (Col. 3:12-17)

Wednesday—Proper Conduct (Eph. 5:1-14)

Thursday—Concern for Others (James 2:14-26)

Friday—Attributes to Manifest (II Peter 1:5-11)

Saturday—Love of the World (I John 2:15-17)

Sunday—Contentment (I Tim. 6:6-11)

The second area in which we see how the provision of our lives is complete in Christ deals with our priorities. We learn much about a person when we find out what he feels is most important in his life. Instead of being content with what we have in Jesus Christ, we often concentrate on the wrong thing and that which is merely temporal in value. Our joy is related much to our being satisfied that in Jesus Christ we already have everything!

> Finally, brethren, whatever is true, whatever is honorable, whatever is right, whatever is pure, whatever is lovely, whatever is of good repute, if there is any excellence and if anything worthy of praise, let your mind dwell on these things. The things you have learned and received and heard and seen in me, practice these things; and the God of peace shall be with you. But I rejoiced in the Lord greatly, that now at last you have revived your concern for me; indeed, you were concerned before, but you lacked opportunity. Not that I speak from want; for I have learned to be content in whatever circumstances I am. I know how to get along with humble means, and I also know how to live in prosperity; in any and every circumstance I have learned the secret of being filled and going hungry, both of having abundance and suffering need. I can do all things through Him who strengthens me (Phil. 4:8-13).

I. AS TO YOUR CONCENTRATION ON IMPORTANT THINGS — 4:8

The first words of verse 8, translated "finally," literally mean "the rest" or "that which remains." Paul summarizes whatever else he might say to them about joy and unity, growing in Christ, by urging them to concentrate on things that manifest certain qualities which he lists in this verse.

A. A DESCRIPTION of what is important.

1. In terms of specific *qualities*. Paul here lists six qualities that should characterize the things that we feel are really important in our lives. If what we do and say and what we think about are centered in these wonderful characteristics, we will discover a greater degree of growth and joy in the Lord than we have previously known.

a. *True*. The little word "whatever" is a relative adjective that can reflect several things. It can refer to space and be translated "as great as." It can refer to time, and be read, "as long as." It can refer to number, and say, "as many as." It can also point to importance and be translated, "how great in value." It seems that the latter would be the proper usage in this verse. The emphasis is on the importance of each of these characteristics or qualities. The word "true" is a combination of the negative "not" and the word "to forget." In contrast to that which is concealed or hidden, that which is "true" is that which is open, honest and manifested to all. The things we do that are the opposite of this should be avoided. We should concentrate on living open, honest lives before others.

b. *Honorable.* This word emphasizes a seriousness of purpose. We could translate it "serious" or "grave" or "reverent." The idea is that of seriousness and dignity. The things that manifest this trait will reveal a seriousness of purpose in the person's life who does them. Too often we are flippant and careless about life and the things we do. God wants us to be serious, not in the sense that we can never smile or laugh, but in the sense of purpose and direction.

c. *Right.* This word emphasizes the state of being right and refers to right conduct. The opposite, of course, is wrong conduct. We often concentrate on that which is sinful and wrong, rather than on what is right and godly.

d. *Pure.* This word is from the root word translated "holy" or "holiness." The basic idea is that of separateness. God is holy in that He is separated from that which is created (He as Creator) and also from that which is sinful or defiled. It is also translated clean or cleanliness. Thinking on that which is "dirty" cannot help our joy and growth in the Lord but only drag us down to the gutter. We are to concentrate on that which separates from sin, not that which leads to sin.

e. *Lovely.* This is a beautiful word. It is a combination of one of the words for "love" and the preposition "toward." We are exhorted to concentrate on that which is toward love. Instead of thinking strife, hostility, resentment, and bitterness, we are to think love and friendship. This word for love is also used as friendship. Do things in your Christian life that build friendships instead of those things that will tear them down. Seek to manifest love toward others instead of hate. Much joy is sacrificed because we fail to do this. There is such a need for love among believers. Many are starving for close friendships with another brother or sister in the Lord, one with whom they can share their burdens.

f. *Good repute.* The root idea of this word is simply "to speak well." To say good things about people instead of criticizing them all the time will greatly enhance your spiritual growth and your joy in the Lord. The average conversation among believers is characterized by judging others and throwing out critical remarks toward others that we would not say if they were in our presence. No wonder there is so little joy in our midst!

2. In terms of *value.* Not only in terms of specific qualities does Paul

describe what is really important, but also in terms of value. He says, "if there is any excellence and if anything worthy of praise." The word "if" sometimes suggests doubt or probability to us. The Greek language has a word for "if" and a construction with it that indicates, "if, and we know it's true." That is what appears here. It is true that there is value in these six qualities Paul mentions. And, since it is true, we are to act upon it. The value of these things is expressed by the usage of two words:

a. *Excellence.* This word emphasizes the moral goodness connected with these six qualities. I Peter 2:9 refers this to God Himself when it says "the excellencies of Him." II Peter 1:5 tells us to supply "moral excellence" in our faith.

b. *Worthy of praise.* This word is used of praise to God and was so used by Paul back in chapter 1, verse 11, when it says, "to the glory and *praise* of God." God is praised when these specific qualities are found in the believer's life.

B. A DUTY we have toward these things.

". . . let your mind dwell on these things." These words simply mean to "think these things." It is not so much to think about them, but to think them! The word "think" is our word "logic." Make these things the logic of your life! What we think about, reveals what we are!

II. AS TO YOUR CONDUCT — 4:9

> The things you have learned and received and heard and seen in me, practice these things; and the God of peace shall be with you.

We cannot divorce what Paul said in verse 8 from what he says in verse 9. Conduct is the natural product of what we think and know. If we are really thinking about the right things, we shall notice the difference in our conduct.

A. The RESPONSIBILITY we have.

". . . practice these things." These words emphasize a continual pattern of life. It is not a suggestion, but a command. What things are involved?

1. Things you have *learned.*
2. Things you have *received.*
3. Things you have *heard.*
4. Things you have *seen.*

All of these things were the results of Paul's life and testimony. He says that they were "in me" and thus, would be familiar as well as obvious to these Philippian believers. We need to be reminded that we cannot teach without example, neither do people learn without a pattern to follow. It is one thing to hear the words, but it is quite another to have learned them by personal experience and example. They "saw" these things in Paul's life as well as "heard" them.

B. The RESULT we can expect.

". . . and the God of peace shall be with you." Paul just finished telling us about God's peace (v. 7), and now he indicates that the God who produces that peace is "with" the person who practices these qualities and thinks about them. It is important that we learn this principle: God's peace is given to those who put into practice the positive qualities of the Christian life and who emphasize what is truly important.

III. AS TO YOUR CONTENTMENT — 4:10-12

> But I rejoiced in the Lord greatly, that now at last you have revived your concern for me; indeed, you were concerned before, but you lacked opportunity. Not that I speak from want; for I have learned to be content in whatever circumstances I am. I know how to get along with humble means, and I also know how to live in prosperity; in any and every circumstance I have learned the secret of being filled and going hungry, both of having abundance and suffering need.

No words could possibly "say it better" in terms of being content! We are so often filled with restlessness, dissatisfaction, and discontent. Our priorities are out of order, and as a result, we have little contentment and thus, little joy. It is important that every believer learn the secret behind these words. We shall not always experience the same level of salary, nor have the same portion of goods or household items. God will often place us in difficult circumstances. Much of the world is currently starving and without what some would call "basic necessities" of life. How important then that we see the principle behind these verses. The theme of chapter 4 is: "The provision of your life is complete in Jesus Christ." Do we really believe that? It is especially hard to understand that principle when we are in "want" and suffering.

A. Seen in Paul's EXPRESSION of joy.

"But I rejoiced in the Lord greatly." It is most difficult to tell others to "rejoice" in all the circumstances of life if you have not learned to do so. Paul wrote out of experience.

1. The *reason* behind it—"that now at last you have revived your con-

cern for me." The word "that" can also be translated "because." It was because of the revival of concern he saw in their lives that he had great joy. The word "now" means "at this time." Paul seems to have been the recipient of a gift from them that showed their concern for him. The word "revived" means "to blossom again." They had shown concern for him previously, but it had evidently been awhile since he had heard from them. The word "concern" simply means "to be thinking" or "to be mindful." It is so refreshing to know that people are thinking of you when you are in difficult circumstances. To be remembered is very important in terms of encouragement and as an expression of love. Many missionaries no doubt would identify readily with what Paul is saying here.

2. The *reference* to their failure to respond earlier. Paul says, "indeed, you were concerned before, but you lacked opportunity." It is beautiful to observe how Paul dealt with people. Truly he had learned from Christ! He deals very gently with a tender subject—their remembrance of him. The word "indeed" could be translated "before which." The idea is that they were concerned before. The words "you lacked opportunity" come from a word meaning "a good season." The point is that the time did not seem right. Paul assumes that they desired to show their love for him but the right moment had not arrived until now. Of course, in God's plan, this was certainly so. God brought the encouragement to Paul just at the time he really needed it.

B. Seen in Paul's EXPERIENCE – 4:11-12.

Contentment is expressed by Paul in his joy over their recent manifestation of love and in the fact that he had not heard from them in a good while. But the basic way we understand the principle of contentment and how it relates to our joy in the Lord is by observing it in Paul's own personal experience.

1. He experienced *contentment*—4:11. "Not that I speak from want; for I have learned to be content in whatever circumstances I am." The word "want" comes from the verb "to be behind." The word "content" carries the idea of the word "sufficient" plus the word for "self." It comes to mean "self-sufficient." In spite of the absence of any one's help or gifts, Paul had learned how to be self-sufficient, trusting upon the Lord to meet his needs. He managed, in other words, to get along, and he was confident of the Lord's supply and provision. David wrote in Psalm 23, "The Lord is my shepherd, I shall not want."

2. He experienced the *contrast* of abundance and want—4:12. Paul was

not speaking out of a life of ease and prosperity. He really knew hardship and deprivation. You can read about his testimony in II Corinthians 11.

a. In *living* with it personally—"I know how to get along with humble means, and I also know how to live in prosperity." In the construction of this sentence we have the repetition of the Greek word "and," and the idea is that of "both . . . and." He knew both sides of the economic ladder. He spoke out of experience. The words "get along with humble means" come from a present infinitive form which means "to be continually humbled." It wasn't a momentary experience that Paul was referring to; he knew suffering in this sense as a pattern of life. It had been a way of existence with him. The words "to live in prosperity" mean "to be continually abounding." Paul also knew life when economically everything was going his way. He had lived with both sides, and thus could speak with experience to all of us.

b. In *learning* how to live with it—"in any and every circumstance I have learned the secret of being filled and going hungry, both of having abundance and suffering need." This is such an all-inclusive statement. Literally, it says, "in every thing and in all things." In each circumstance and in all the various positions of life, Paul had learned the secret of contentment. The words "I have learned the secret" are very fascinating. They refer to being initiated into the mysteries. There were many so-called "mystery religions" in that day. Paul used the example of one who is initiated into them and their secrets in referring to what he had learned about contentment. It is very appropriate when you think about it because that is the real problem. To many of us it is still a mystery! We have had many possessions and have been without them, and yet, so many of us, have never learned the secret of contentment. Paul again puts two things in contrast to one another. They are opposites in Greek. "Being filled" is the opposite of "going hungry." The word for "being filled" means "to satisfy with food; to feed; to fatten animals." It is the direct opposite of going hungry—not having anything to eat. Paul knew what it was to have more than enough to eat, and he knew what it was to be hungry for just some kind of food no matter what it was.

Just what is the secret of contentment? Many young couples ruin their lives by a continual desire for "things" that they hope will bring them happiness. Note the powerful words that Paul wrote on this subject to the young man Timothy (I Tim. 6:6-10).

But godliness actually is a means of great gain, when accompanied by contentment. For we have brought nothing into the world, so we cannot take anything out of it either. And if we have food and covering, with these we shall be content. But those who want to get rich fall into temptation and a snare and many foolish and harmful desires which plunge men into ruin and destruction. For the love of money is a root of all sorts of evil, and some by longing for it have wandered away from the faith, and pierced themselves with many a pang.

It seems that we could summarize the doctrine of contentment from these verses by observing the following things:

(1) Contentment comes when we recognize how we came into the world and how we will go out of the world. The old saying goes, "You can't take it with you." People even put valuable possessions into the coffins of dead loved ones. This followed the pattern of the ancient Egyptians who prepared places where they would be buried by filling them with many possessions that they thought they would use and need in the "after life."

(2) Contentment is lost when we desire to get rich. It is not simply the rich to whom Paul is speaking, but those "who want to get rich." If God gives you wealth to use for His glory, praise the Lord! But do not seek it—it will destroy you and at the very least, rob you of contentment and joy.

(3) Contentment refuses to love money and possessions. Jesus said: "Where your treasure is, there will your heart be also" (Matt. 6:21). The "love of the world" is fighting against our "love for God" (cf. I John 2:15-17). In addition to these things, we could add a fourth fact.

(4) Contentment is found when we realize that the things of this life do not bring happiness and will not last. The "world" is passing away. The "treasures on earth" will rust and decay. We are admonished to "lay up treasures in heaven." Money can be used to glorify God when it is invested in God's work and purposes on earth. So many of us fail to have contentment because we ignore these basic principles of the Word of God. The "things" of this world will not bring us happiness. Augustine (church father) said: "Two verbs have built two empires. The verb 'to have' and the verb 'to be.' 'To have' is the world of things. 'To be' is the world of our character. It is more important to be what God wants me to be than to have all of life's possessions and fame."

IV.   AS TO YOUR CONFIDENCE — 4:13

"I can do all things through Him who strengthens me." Here is the summary and the secret! In Christ we have the strength to do all things! Perfect contentment is found when we learn that in Christ we have all we need! The songwriter who wrote "Satisfied" knew this principle when he said:

> All my life long I had panted for a drop from some clear spring; that I hoped would quench the burning of the thirst I felt within. Hallelujah! I have found Him whom my soul so long has craved! Jesus satisfies my longings; through His blood I now am saved!

A. The STRENGTH involved.

There are several words translated "strength" or "strong." The word used here which is translated "I can do" emphasizes inherent strength or ability. It does not mean that we in ourselves have this ability as the rest of the verse clearly explains. It is God's strength in us that gives us this ability to do "all things." How great is the provision of the life in Christ!

B. The SCOPE of it.

"All things." It is easy to relegate the "big" decisions and works to God, and to take on the small ones ourselves. The Bible emphasizes "all things." We need God's strength in every circumstance of life.

C. The SOURCE of it.

". . . through Him who strengthens me." These words literally translated are, "in the one empowering me," or "in the one giving me the power," or "by means of the one putting power within me." The idea should be clear. The ability to do "all things" is the result of having God's power put within us. The King James Version interprets this as referring to Christ. Certainly it is "Christ in you" which is the secret to victorious living. It could also refer to the ministry of the Holy Spirit whom the Bible does say gives us power.

The provision of our life is complete in Christ—nothing is lacking. We must learn to concentrate on what is really important and learn to be content in all circumstances of life, knowing that God will meet our needs.

STUDY QUESTIONS:

1. What qualities should characterize the things we do and say?
2. What is the meaning of "contentment" according to these verses?
3. How does one have the ability to do "all things"?

13   PHILIPPIANS 4:14-23

+++

Your Advantages
With God's Provision

+++

THE CHAPTER OUTLINED:

    I. Seen in Their Example
      A. In his affliction
      B. In his association with them
      C. In his absence from them

    II. Seen in the Experience of Paul
      A. As to his personal desires
      B. As to his description of how God met his needs

    III. Seen in the Extent to which God Will Meet Our Needs
      A. As to source
      B. As to scope
      C. As to supply
      D. As to submission

SUGGESTED BACKGROUND DEVOTIONAL READING

Monday—Sharing Afflictions (I Peter 4:12-19)

Tuesday—Example of Giving (II Cor. 8:1-5)

Wednesday—Willingness to Give (II Cor. 8:6-12)

Thursday—Abundance and Want (II Cor. 8:13-24)

Friday—How to Give (II Cor. 9:1-7)

Saturday—Supplying Our Need (II Cor. 9:9-15)

Sunday—Praising God for Others (Col. 4:7-18)

The last few verses of the previous discussion told us of Paul's great contentment in life. He knew both sides of the economic ladder. He knew how to live in prosperity and how to get along with humble means. He again expresses that thought in these closing verses of the epistle, but makes special comment to the Philippians about their example of concern and giving.

> Nevertheless, you have done well to share with me in my affliction. And you yourselves also know, Philippians, that at the first preaching of the gospel, after I departed from Macedonia, no church shared with me in the matter of giving and receiving but you alone; for even in Thessalonica you sent a gift more than once for my needs. Not that I seek the gift itself, but I seek for the profit which increases to your account. But I have received everything in full, and have an abundance; I am amply supplied, having received from Epaphroditus what you have sent, a fragrant aroma, an acceptable sacrifice, well pleasing to God. And my God shall supply all your needs according to His riches in glory in Christ Jesus. Now to our God and Father be the glory forever and ever. Amen. Greet every saint in Christ Jesus. The brethren who are with me greet you. All the saints greet you, especially those of Caesar's household. The grace of the Lord Jesus Christ be with your spirit (Phil. 4:14-23).

I. SEEN IN THEIR EXAMPLE — 4:14-16

The first word of verse 14, "nevertheless," connects the previous verses to this one. Paul would be saying by this that in spite of his knowing how to get along without anyone's help and thus, being content, these Philippian believers had helped him for which he was most grateful. He is commending them for their concern for him even though he wanted to make it clear that God was taking care of him and that he had learned to trust God in all circumstances of life. This church above any others demonstrated their love for the Apostle Paul and their concern for his material needs.

A. In his AFFLICTION — 4:14.

> Nevertheless, you have done well to share with me in my affliction.

1. The *manner* in which they shared with him—"you have done well." The aorist tense of the verb would point to a particular act. Paul is referring to a particular gift they shared with him. He is commending them for doing "well" not because it was he who received the gift, but because they were willing to share.

2. The *meaning* of this act of sharing—"to share with me." The word translated "share" comes first of all from the word often translated "fel-

lowship" and from the preposition "with." To "fellowship" is "to share in common." There is a fellowship of possessions referred to in the Word of God (Rom. 12:13—"*contributing* to the needs of the saints"). The preposition "with" only strengthens the word to emphasize that these Philippian believers were willing to share what they had with Paul. It is the spirit and attitude behind this gift which is so commendable.

B. In his ASSOCIATION with them — 4:15.

> And you yourselves also know, Philippians, that at the first preaching of the gospel, after I departed from Macedonia, no church shared with me in the matter of giving and receiving but you alone.

1. The *facts* were known to them and they responded—"you yourselves also know." The word "know" tells us that they knew the facts behind Paul's first visit, and that they were the only church to help in Paul's support.

2. The *failure* of others to help. It was not easy for Paul to speak these words, but they were the facts. We see a side of Paul's personality that helps us to understand that he is human like the rest of us. It reveals that he was often alone in his ministry with very little evidence of others really caring about him and his needs. It would have been so much more encouraging to have had each church respond spontaneously to his needs. But as it worked out in God's plan, Paul was the one who had to tell them how to give and how to support God's workers. What a joy, then, for Paul to have had this church respond so willingly to his needs! No wonder they held such a special place in his heart!

a. The *circumstances* involved—"after I departed from Macedonia" and "that at the first [beginning] preaching of the gospel." Paul is not talking about how this church gave to him while he was there, but after he left. Even after such a short visit (the first time—Acts 16) they still cared enough to send a little help to him as he went on his journey. After all, that's when he really needed the help—when he went for the "first" time into these cities with the Gospel. It reminds us of how much our missionaries today need our support.

b. The *character* of this help—"shared with me in the matter of giving and receiving." Paul is alluding here to the principle he mentioned in Galatians 6:6: "And let the one who is taught the word share all good things with him who teaches." It is the same idea found in I Corinthians 9:11-14. The "giving" is the response of those who have heard the Word. The "receiving" is the result of those preaching the Word. If we have "received" spiritual food, we should "give" materially to the support of those who shared it with us.

c. The *contrast* with the Philippians—"but you alone." Others had failed to support the ministry of Paul and his missionary team, but not the Philippians. This was the only church to respond. Paul uses their example to give his tremendous teaching on giving in II Corinthians 8 and 9. It was these "Macedonian believers" whom he used as an example to motivate the Corinthian believers to give.

C. In his ABSENCE from them – 4:16.

> ... for even in Thessalonica you sent a gift more than once for my needs.

1. The *place* where he experienced their concern—"Thessalonica." In studying the passage in Acts 17:1-15, we can immediately see that there was much opposition to the Gospel when Paul came to Thessalonica. While some did respond to the Gospel, many Jews became "upset" and began to stir up trouble. They even followed him down to Berea, and the believers had to send Paul away by night. What a blessing then to know that the Philippian believers were sending gifts to him at this time of trouble and need! What an encouragement it must have been!

2. The *pattern* they established—"you sent more than once." We are often compelled to give at least once to some cause or some worthy person, but the real test of our concern is how much we continue to support that project or that person. These believers were faithful in their giving and continued to support the Apostle Paul.

3. The *purpose* they had—"for my needs." It is important that the believers learn of the needs of the workers in order to meet those needs. Their motivation was to help Paul, and it is a worthy motivation. Every time we give to others, we are giving to Christ, and not even a "cup of cold water" given in His name will go unnoticed by Him. When our motivation is right, there is reward. It is always right to give in order to meet the needs of another person. Ephesians 4:28 states, "Let him who steals steal no longer; but rather let him labor, performing with his own hands what is good, in order that he may have something to share with him who has need." James 2:15-17 says:

> If a brother or sister is without clothing and in need of daily food, and one of you says to them, "Go in peace, be warmed and be filled"; and yet you do not give them what is necessary for their body; what use is that? Even so faith, if it has no works, is dead, being by itself.

II. SEEN IN THE EXPERIENCE OF PAUL — 4:17-18

Not only do we see the advantages of God's provision in the example of the Philippian believers, but we see it also in the personal experience of Paul.

A. As to his personal DESIRES — 4:17.

> Not that I seek the gift itself, but I seek for the profit which increases to your account.

His personal desires fall into two areas: their gift and their growth in the Lord.

1. Regarding their *gift*—"Not that I seek the gift itself." The word "seek" is a strong word. Paul is saying that he was not setting his heart on receiving the gift that they had sent. It was not for the reason that he wanted more money or more support that he gave these words. It was to profit them. When you teach someone how to give, you are blessing their lives. They will reap the benefits and the joy from the Lord in the matter of their giving.

2. Regarding their *growth*—"but I seek for the profit which increases to your account." The word "profit" is the word "fruit."

a. The *blessing* of it—"increases." You can never "out-give" God! The "fruit" of their lives will continue to increase because of their gift. It will become a great blessing in their lives.

b. The *benefit* of it—"to your account." The word "account" is the word usually translated "word." It is closely related to the word meaning "account" or to "count" something to be so, or "reason." The point is that their pattern of giving will accrue to their own personal account in terms of spiritual growth.

B. As to his DESCRIPTION of how God met his needs — 4:18.

> But I have received everything in full, and have an abundance; I am amply supplied, having received from Epaphroditus what you have sent, a fragrant aroma, an acceptable sacrifice, well pleasing to God.

1. The *contentment* he had—"But I have received everything in full, and have an abundance." Paul always displayed a contentment with the way in which God was meeting his needs. He expresses to these believers that he is not writing these words because he has a particular need at this time. He emphasizes that by telling them that he has an "abundance" which literally means, "I am continuing to abound."

2. The *coming* of Epaphroditus—"I am amply supplied, having received

from Epaphroditus what you have sent." In chapter 2 of this epistle, verses 25-30, we have already learned of the dedication and commitment of Epaphroditus, whom Paul described in Philippians 2:25 as "your messenger and minister to my need."

a. The *supply* involved—"I am amply supplied." These words come from a verb in the perfect tense which means "I have been made full." The perfect tense refers to a past fact that has present finished results. Paul is saying that he did receive the gift, and as a result, he is still well supplied.

b. The *sending* of it—"what you have sent." Literally, it says, "the things from you." Epaphroditus brought it, but Paul emphasizes the source of it. It was sent by these believers, thus indicating their love and concern for Paul in his time of need.

3. The *character* of their gift—"a fragrant aroma [offering], an acceptable sacrifice, well pleasing to God." Notice three things about this gift which the Philippian believers sent.

a. The *smell*—"a fragrant aroma." These words remind us of chapter 4, verse 2, where one of the ladies mentioned in that verse, Euodia, has a name with the same letters. We mentioned in our study of Philippians 4:2 that her name could mean "a good [well] journey." It could also mean a "good smell." Paul wrote in II Corinthians 2:15-16: "For we are a fragrance of Christ to God among those who are being saved and among those who are perishing; to the one an aroma from death to death, to the other an aroma from life to life. And who is adequate for these things?" The word "fragrance" is the same word used in Philippians 4:18, when it translates "fragrant." The word "aroma" is the same in both passages. Not only are believers a "good smell" but so also their acts of giving.

b. The *sacrifice*—"an acceptable sacrifice." The word "acceptable" is simply an adjective from the verb meaning "to receive or accept." It refers to a person or thing that has been regarded favorable. The gift of these Philippian believers is like a sacrifice that has been accepted by God. Romans 12:1 reminds us that our lives are to be like "sacrifices" to God which we are to present to Him.

c. The *satisfaction* to God—"well pleasing to God." God is pleased with this kind of giving. Our basic motivation in our Christian life ought to be to please God in all we do. When we share our possessions with someone else who is in need, God is pleased with our gift.

III. SEEN IN THE EXTENT TO WHICH GOD WILL MEET OUR NEEDS — 4:19-20

The third way in which we see the advantages of God's wonderful provision is in the way God meets our needs. We never have to worry about Him taking care of us. Often we question whether we should give to someone in need because we might jeopardize our own financial situation. If you want the advice that Jesus gave on this matter, read Luke 6:38.

A. As to SOURCE — "And my God."

We need to recognize that the source behind the supply of all our needs is God Almighty! He owns everything! How can we go wrong when we trust ourselves to Him. I Corinthians 4:7 says: "And what do you have that you did not receive? But if you did receive it, why do you boast as if you had not received it?" Everything we have comes from God (cf. James 1:17; Ps. 24:1). How foolish that we would doubt that God could take care of us!

B. As to SCOPE — "all your needs."

Literally it reads, "every need of yours." There is not one thing that God cannot do or cannot supply. He knows your needs even before you ask Him. He can supply your every need! Trust Him!

C. As to SUPPLY — "according to His riches in glory in Christ Jesus."

That supply, friends, will never run out! This is kind of a favorite expression of Paul. He mentions something similar to this in Ephesians 1:7, 18; 2:7; 3:8, 16; and Colossians 1:27.

1. The *place* where these riches are found—"in glory." This would probably refer to the "glory of God Himself." The point would be that God Himself is the source as well as the supply, and His infinite life makes it all possible. He owns everything, and in Himself He is everything!

2. The *Person* who makes it possible—"in Christ Jesus." The "glory of God" is in Jesus Christ (II Cor. 4:6) and He is God (Col. 2:9) and thus "all the fulness" of God. This reminds us of Ephesians 1:3 where it says, "Blessed be the God and Father of our Lord Jesus Christ, who has blessed us with every spiritual blessing in the heavenly places in Christ." We have everything we need when we are "in Christ"! Nothing is missing!

D. As to SUBMISSION — 4:20. "Now to our God and Father be the glory forever and ever. Amen."

The purpose of this statement is not simply to close the epistle on a triumphant note. From the context it appears that the previous verse (19) was so personally exciting to Paul that he could not do anything else but praise God! Knowing that God will supply all our need and that His supply is limitless, we can do nothing else but bow to Him and give Him all the glory and all the praise! Notice that He deserves all the glory "forever and ever." We shall continue to praise God for all eternity! Read the wonderful verses in the Book of Revelation, chapter 5, verses 9, 12-13, and now read Revelation 4:11. There doesn't seem to be any question about God's desire to receive glory and honor and praise. He wants us to praise and thank Him for all He has done, is doing, and shall do! Paul concludes this great verse with the word "Amen," and so do we!

FINAL WORDS OF GREETING

The last three verses are in many ways like other epistles of Paul and unless closely observed, would not appear to be unusual in any way. However, upon close scrutiny, we do find quite an amazing statement! The word "greet" bears no unusual significance, and, of course, was the common way to end a letter. It was a technical term for conveying greetings at the close of a letter, very often by an amanuensis, that is, a secretary employed to do the writing for you. Paul uses the word three times in these verses.

(1) *The believers in Philippi*—"Greet every saint in Christ Jesus" (4:21). The word "saint" refers to a believer, one set apart by God for Himself and His use. Paul did not want anyone of the believers in Philippi to feel excluded from his greetings, so he used the word "every."

(2) *The brothers with Paul*—"The brethren who are with me greet you" (4:21). This would certainly include Timothy (Phil. 1:1, 2:19) and Epaphroditus (Phil. 2:25; 4:18). It might also include Tychicus (Eph. 6:21), Epaphras (Col. 4:12), Onesimus (Col. 4:9), Aristarchus, Mark, and Justus (Col. 4:10-11), and Luke and Demas (Col. 4:14).

(3) *The background of those in Rome*—"All the saints greet you, especially those of Caesar's household" (4:22). Now this is the unusual statement to which we previously referred—"Caesar's household." The word "especially" means "most of all" or "above all." Paul was emphasizing how the Lord had worked through his imprisonment at Rome. He saved the best news until the last! Compare this statement with his earlier words in Philippians 1:12-13. Most scholars hold that Paul was in prison in Rome at the time that Nero was the emperor. The date of Paul's imprison-

ment there was probably around A.D. 63-64. Nero had Rome burned in A.D. 64 and blamed the fire on the Christians. Nero murdered several members of his own family for their faith in Christianity. Paul makes this simple yet glorious statement—"All the saints greet you, especially those of Caesar's household." What a testimony! Paul's influence was so powerful that members of Caesar's own family had come to know Jesus Christ as Saviour! Praise the Lord! No wonder Paul told them not to be discouraged or saddened over his present circumstances! God was using him in a mighty way! In Ephesians 6:10-17, Paul describes the armor of a Roman soldier and applies it to the Christian life. Could it be that he was winning those soldiers to Christ who had to stand guard over him? They then were taking the "good news" of Christ all over the Praetorian guard house. As a result, members of Nero's family became Christians. Although the details and circumstances cannot be known for sure, we know one thing for sure—members of Nero's household had become Christians, and that is something to praise God for and a basis of rejoicing!

(4) *The blessing from God*—"The grace of the Lord Jesus Christ be with your spirit" (4:23). Such a beautiful way to close a letter! God's wonderful grace is all we need! The word "be" is supplied and could just as easily be the word "is." Instead of a wish or prayer, it could be a statement of fact—"the grace of our Lord Jesus Christ *is* with your spirit."

What a wonderful letter—a letter of joy! Our lives should be different because of reading this and studying it in depth. No matter what the circumstances of our lives and the problems we face, we can have the joy of the Lord! We end with that challenging verse of chapter 4:

"Rejoice in the Lord always; again I will say, rejoice!"

STUDY QUESTIONS:

1. What lessons did you learn from the example of giving that these Philippian believers displayed?

2. How did Paul describe the gift of these Philippian believers?

3. What principles did you learn from Philippians 4:19?

4. What amazing fact is found in the final greeting?

Bibliography

Blair, J. Allen. *Living Victoriously.* Grand Rapids: Wm. B. Eerdmans Publishing Co., 1956.

Eadie, John. *Commentary on the Greek Text of the Epistle of Paul to the Philippians.* Grand Rapids: Zondervan Publishing House, 1859.

Harrison, Norman Baldwin. *His In Joyous Experience.* Minneapolis: Harrison Service, 1926.

Hendricksen, William. *A Commentary on the Epistle to the Philippians.* Grand Rapids: Baker Book House, 1962.

Ironside, Harry A. *Notes on Philippians.* New York: Loizeaux Brothers, 1922.

King, Guy H. *Joy Way.* London: Marshall, Morgan, and Scott, 1952.

Laurin, Roy L. *Life Advances!* Published by author, 1943.

Lenski, R. C. H. *Interpretation of St. Paul's Epistles to the Galatians, to the Ephesians, and to the Philippians.* Minneapolis: Augsburg Publishing House, 1961.

Lightfoot, Joseph Barber. *St. Paul's Epistle to the Philippians.* Grand Rapids: Zondervan Publishing House, n.d.

Martin, Ralph P. *The Epistle of Paul to the Philippians.* Grand Rapids: Wm. B. Eerdmans Publishing Co., 1959.

McClain, Alva J. *Sermons on Philippians.* Unpublished notes, 1920.

Meyer, F. B. *The Epistle to the Philippians.* London: Marshall, Morgan, and Scott, 1952.

Moule, H. C. G. *Philippian Studies.* London: Hodden and Stroughton, 1897.

Robertson, A. T. *Paul's Joy in Christ.* Westwood, New Jersey: Fleming Revell Publishing Co., 1927.

Strauss, Lehman. *Devotional Studies in Philippians.* New York: Loizeaux Brothers, 1959.

Tenney, Merrill C. *Philippians.* Grand Rapids: Wm. B. Eerdmans Publishing Co., 1956.

Vincent, Marvin R. *A Critical and Exegetical Commentary on the Epistle to the Philippians and to Philemon.* New York: Charles Scribner's Sons, 1897.

Vine, W. E. *Epistles to the Philippians and Colossians.* London: Oliphants, 1955.

Walvoord, John F. *Philippians: Triumph in Christ.* Chicago: Moody Press, 1971.

Wuest, Kenneth S. *Philippians in the Greek New Testament.* Grand Rapids: Wm. B. Eerdmans Publishing Co. 1942.